Osprey Modelling • 43

Modelling Armoured Vehicles

G Edmundson, J Carswell, T Cockle, G Davidson
& S van Beveren

Consultant editor Robert Oehler • *Series editors* Marcus Cowper and Nikolai Bogdanovic

First published in Great Britain in 2008 by Osprey Publishing,
Midland House, West Way, Botley, Oxford OX2 0PH, UK
44-02 23rd St, Suite 219, Long Island City, NY 11101, USA
Email: info@ospreypublishing.com

Osprey Publishing is part of the Osprey Group.

Transferred to digital print on demand 2011

First published 2008
1st impression 2008

Printed and bound by PrintOnDemand-Worldwide.com, Peterborough, UK

A CIP catalogue record for this book is available from the British Library

ISBN: 978 1 84603 287 5

Editorial by Ilios Publishing Ltd, Oxford, UK (www.iliospublishing.com)
Index by Michael Forder
Design by Servis Filmsetting Ltd, Stockport, Cheshire
Typeset in GillSans and Stone Serif
Originated by PPS Grasmere Ltd, Leeds, UK

The Woodland Trust
Osprey Publishing is supporting the Woodland Trust, the UK's leading woodland
conservation charity, by funding the dedication of trees.

www.ospreypublishing.com

Contents

Introduction

Tamiya's Char B1 bis kit was built with help of some after-market accessories to improve the detail and accuracy.

The finished model incorporated many painting and weathering steps to achieve a realistic appearance.

This book has been written primarily for modellers of a skill level of beginner to intermediate, and demonstrates techniques that can take their AFV modelling projects to a higher level of accuracy, detail and appeal. Unlike other titles in the Osprey Modelling Series, this book focuses on techniques rather than how to model specific vehicles. It describes how to conduct preliminary project research and provides tips on basic and advanced levels of construction. Painting, marking and weathering a model are demonstrated, along with various ideas for presenting a finished model with figures in a vignette or diorama. All of the work in the book has been done in 1/35 scale, but the methods demonstrated would apply to models of any scale.

Five contributors have combined their efforts to present the reader with varied approaches to modelling. The projects chosen and the methods demonstrated cover a wide range of subject matter and skills.

Gary Edmundson shows basic model construction and also adds a few after-market parts to a Tamiya Char B1 bis, which is presented along with a second model in a diorama. France produced 369 Char B1 bis tanks between April 1937 and June 1940. Developed in the 1920s, the tank resembled World War I tanks, with track runs that went around the entire outside of the hull and the running gear protected by the side armour plate. Although the B1 bis was well armed with a 75mm gun and thick armour, it was not available in sufficient numbers and suffered from poor tactical employment during the German invasion of 1940. Gary's model represents vehicle number '448' named 'Nancy II', which served with the 37e Bataillon de Chars de Combat (BCC), and was lost during the fighting in Belgium in May 1940.

Materials used

Tamiya: French Battle Tank B1 bis kit 35282

Blast Models: BL350103K Update set for B1 BIS French Version – Tamiya

Friulmodel: B1-Bis white-metal individual track links ATL-88

Lion Roar: Etched-metal detail set for Tamiya B1 bis including turned aluminium gun barrels LE35075

Echelon Fine Details: Decal sheet for Chars B1 bis of the 37e BCC tanks sheet number ALT352004

Evergreen styrene in sheet, rod and tube

Tamiya acrylic paints: XF-57 Buff; XF-1 Flat Black; XF-64 Red Brown; XF-7 Flat Red; XF-58 Olive Green; X-22 Clear Gloss

MIG Productions' pigments: Black Smoke P023; Europe Dust P028

Rembrandt chalk pastels: Raw Umber, Yellow Ochre, Orange, Burnt Umber, Black

Floquil Railroad colours: F110017 Weathered Black; F110070 Roof Brown

Humbrol enamels: 11 Silver; 53 Steel; 72 Khaki Drill; 29 Dark Earth

Lifecolor Tensocrom acrylics: Oil TSC 207

Winsor & Newton oil paints: Raw Umber 554; Ivory Black 331

Jim Carswell created a small vignette by adding figures and a partial interior to Trumpeter's LAV-25 kit. The LAV-25 (Light Armoured Vehicle – 25mm gun turret) has been in service with the United States Marine Corps since the mid-1980s. By the time of the early stages of Operation *Iraqi Freedom* phase 1 (OIF 1) in 2003, many of the LAV-25s used had been modified with at least some of the SLEP upgrades. The SLEP (Service Life Extension Program) upgrades include among other things an improved gunner's thermal sight with armoured housing, scissors-type mount for the M-240G machine gun on the turret, driver's external display, larger exhaust shroud and wider tyres. Externally, as far as the modeller is concerned, it appears LAVs in OIF would at least have the new sight and scissors mount, while the larger exhaust shroud and wider tyres would appear later on in the conflict. As no conversion parts are available for the modeller at the time of writing, some scratch-building is required to build an accurate LAV-25 in OIF.

Wheeled armoured vehicles present their own unique modelling opportunities. Here we see the Trumpeter 1/35-scale USMC LAV-25 (Light Armoured Vehicle – 25mm gun) as seen in the early stages of Operation *Iraqi Freedom*, c.2003.

Modern American vehicles are literally covered with extra stowage. Here are the contents of a stowage set made for the LAV by the company Legend. Only a few of these items will be chosen.

Materials used
Trumpeter: USMC LAV-25 kit 00349
Maple Leaf Models: Early LAV tires MLM 1007; Spare LAV tire MLM 1009
Italeri: LAV-25 (for interior pieces) 259
Legend Productions: LAV-25 Stowage Set LF1113
Lion Roar: LAV-25 photo-etched detail set LE35062
Voyager Model: LAV-25 photo-etched detail set PE35078
Gunze Sangyo: Mr Surfacer 500
Warriors: USMC LAV-25 Crew Pt. 1 and 2, WA35593 and 35594
DML: Modern Machine Gun Set 806
Evergreen: styrene in sheet, rod and tube
Aves: Apoxie Sculpt
Tamiya acrylic paints: XF-67 NATO Green, XF-65 Field Grey, XF-64 Red Brown, XF-69
  NATO Black, XF-57 Buff
Vallejo: acrylics for figures
Humbrol and Model Master: enamels for brush-painted details

To demonstrate methods of dealing with resin kits Tom Cockle constructed a Panzerbefehlswagen III from Cromwell Models. The Panzerbefehlswagen III Ausf. D1 (armoured command vehicle) was built on the same basic chassis as the Panzerkampfwagen III Ausf. D and provided more room for the command staff and radio equipment than the kleine Panzerbefehlswagen I Ausf. B. They

This 1/35-scale Panzerbefehlswagen III Ausf. D was built from a kit consisting of all resin parts. When in the painting stages, the road wheels were simply dry-brushed with black artist's oil paint on the wearing surfaces. This eliminated the need to paint each rubber wheel separately.

were fitted with a FuG 6 plus either a FuG 7 or FuG 8 radio set along with a distinctive frame antenna mounted on the engine deck plus a telescopic eight-metre mast antenna that could be raised through a port in the turret roof. The turret ring was cut out to match the base of the turret and the turret was bolted in place. A dummy 3.7cm gun replaced the original main armament to provide additional space inside the turret leaving only one MG34 mounted in a ball mount in the mantlet for self-protection.

Materials used

Cromwell Models: Panzerbefehlswagen III Ausf. D1 kit LR6
Tristar: Panzerkampfwagen IV Ausf. D kit 015
Modelkasten: SK-57 Pz.IV Early 38cm tracks
Spare tools and antenna from DML Pz.Kpfw.III Ausf. J kit 6394
Evergreen: styrene sheet, strip, tube and rod
Lifecolor acrylic paints: UA207 RAL 7021 Schwarzgrau Panzergrau acrylic paint
Tamiya acrylic paints: XF-52 Flat Earth; XF-51 Khaki Drab; XF-57 Buff; X-25 Clear Green
MIG Productions' pigments: European Dust P028
Humbrol enamels: 29 Matt Dark Earth; HS217 Steel; 160 German Camouflage Red Brown and 187 Sand
Rembrandt pastel chalks: 408-3, 408-7, 234-3 and 409-7
Smooth-On: Mold Max 30 two-part room temperature vulcanizing rubber; Smooth-Cast 300 White Liquid Plastic
Verlinden: resin cobblestone street
DML: 'German Tank Crew 1939-1943' kit 6375

Steve van Beveren converted a DML Panther G kit into an early version of the Jagdpanther. Steve's build features a description of the *Zimmerit* anti-magnetic paste application to the model's hull. The lethal 8.8cm Pak 43/3 gun was mated to a modified Panther chassis to provide the German military with a powerful assault gun. Together these proved to be an effective combination with almost 400 being produced from October 1943 up to April 1945. The Jagdpanther served on both the Eastern and Western fronts with the first unit to receive them being schwere Heeres Panzerjaeger Abteilung 654.

Materials used
DML: Sd.Kfz.171 Panther G Late Production kit 6268
Modelkasten: Panther Late Model Workable Track Set SK-010
Voyager Models: Panther Ausf. G PE35140
Armorscale: 88mm PaK 43/2 L/71 Gun Barrel for German Tank Hunter Jagdpanther
  (Early model) B35-025
Adlers Nest: 7.62mm MG34 (late) Tank Barrel ANM-35002
Evergreen styrene: Sheet
Copper sheet: 0.005in. thick
Aluminium sheet: 0.010in. thick
Prismacolor pencil: HB, silver
Gunze acrylic paints: Oil H342
Tamiya acrylic paints: XF-60 Dark Yellow; XF-63 German Grey; XF-53 Neutral Grey;
  XF-57 Buff; XF-52 Flat Earth; XF-1 Flat Black
Vallejo Air: Dark Yellow 025; Radome Tan 074; Tank Brown 041; Panzer Olive Green 1943
  096; White 001
Vallejo Model Color: Dark Yellow 978; Buff 976; Chocolate Brown 872; Hull Red 985
Humbrol enamels: Pale Yellow 081; Ochre 083
Humbrol Metalcote: Polished Steel 27003
MIG Productions' pigments: Beach Sand P030; Europe Dust P028; Light Dust P027;
  Light Rust P024; Standard Rust P025; Black Smoke P023; Brick Dust P029

Steve van Beveren's conversion of a DML Panther Ausf. G. kit resulted in this early version of the Jagdpanther, built to represent the vehicle currently on display at the Imperial War Museum in London.

Graeme Davidson modified an Academy M981, converting it to a Canadian M113 TUA using some skilful scratch-building techniques. The tube-launched, optically tracked, wire-guided missile (TOW) was designed to give a mechanized infantry unit the ability to counter armoured forces. In Canada, the TOW under armour utilized a twin-missile launcher mated to a modified M113A2 hull. The Canadian Army purchased 72 of these vehicles, with deliveries starting in 1990. The M113 TUA saw combat service in Bosnia with UNPROFOR and SFOR, and later in Kosovo with KFOR.

The majority of the armament for the TUA model was hand-built from styrene stock

The finished model represents a vehicle serving with the Canadian Armed Forces in Bosnia. A wash of MIG Productions pigments was allowed to collect in the recesses of the detail, especially the non-skid surfaces. These tend to trap the mud on the real vehicle.

References and Planning

The production of model kits is sometimes simplified and occasionally the manufacturer can make a mistake in design, which can result in inaccuracies and poor detail. Reference material can guide the modeller to correct some of these problems.

Although limited and often inaccurate, a primary reference for a modeller is the instruction sheet and box art that came with the kit. Model instruction sheets tend to be vague on how and where the parts should be oriented, and some good photographs and drawings certainly can help to overcome this dilemma.

References for the chosen subject should be checked and compared to the model kit. Additional parts and accessories required, such as after-market tracks, decals and conversion sets, can be investigated and planned into the construction. The camouflage scheme in which the model will be finished can also be decided upon.

If the kit offers optional parts for different variants, the specific subject chosen can be referenced to determine which parts will be appropriate. The instruction sheet should be studied closely to understand clearly the construction sequences and orientation of the parts. Instruction sheets are often sequenced according to convenience of illustration, and not in the best sequence for the build. Parts such as the antennae and other small details are best left to the end of the construction to avoid the chance of breaking them.

Proper references are essential when beginning any modelling project, even more so when the subject is a relatively obscure vehicle like the Panzerbefehlswagen III Ausf. DI.

The question of whether to add figures or interior parts to the model should be decided upon early in the process, especially if the final build is to be placed in a diorama or vignette. If there is any interior detailing to carry out, the construction sequence should be altered to accommodate some painting steps prior to the final stages. Plans to add on-vehicle stowage to the kit such as ammunition boxes, fuel containers, tarpaulins and tools should also be determined at this stage.

Modelling AFV kits requires a series of compromises, since no one can ever build the perfect model. Modellers can get bogged down in researching a project so much that the kit is never completed. It is important to strike a balance between pursuing detail and accuracy, and enjoying the satisfaction of completing a model.

Sources of reference

A small fortune can be spent on an AFV reference library. There are countless books and magazines on the subject of tanks and modelling them. By far the most available and affordable sources of reference material are modelling magazines. Several publishers produce magazines focusing on AFV miniatures. There are a number of titles from England, namely *Military Modelling, Military in Scale, Military Modelcraft International, Model Military International* and *AFV Modeller. Military Miniatures in Review* is published in the United States, and written by AFV modellers, providing valuable content for the reader. *Steel Masters* is produced in Paris and, although totally in French, the articles feature modelling projects that are beautifully photographed and laid out. There are also two publications from Spain called *Euro Modelismo* and *Xtreme Modelling* that feature the work of some of the world's top AFV modellers. Several Japanese publications, such as *Armour Modelling* and *Panzer Graph*, provide modelling articles that feature excellent how-to steps including some English captioning. A small number of these magazines can be picked up at a local newsstand, and a greater majority at a well-stocked hobby shop. Either subscription or mail and email order makes the foreign titles easier to come by.

Reference books on AFVs and modelling vary from general titles to specific works on certain vehicle types. The general titles can often be found in local bookshops, but the more focused works are typically found in specialized bookshops and on the Internet. Several series of books have been produced that cover ranges of AFVs in extreme detail, including wartime records, period photos, factory drawings, scale drawings, detailed sketches, photos from surviving examples and battle reports from crew members. Model shows and conventions such as the IPMS Nationals, Euromilitaire and AMPS Nationals in the US bring together vendors that sell these types of books.

Military museums, particularly those containing examples of AFVs, exist in all corners of the world. Modellers should take the opportunity to visit some of the well-populated facilities when travelling nearby and take pictures of their own. Some of the most noteworthy to visit include the Aberdeen Proving Ground in Maryland, USA, the Musée des Blindés in Saumur, France, Bovington Camp in Dorset, The Panzer Museum in Münster, Germany, and the collection at Kubinka near Moscow, Russia.

Model Clubs can be found in larger cities, and usually meet monthly at a community centre. Modellers can share information, provide references and ideas, and inspire one another to achieve higher levels of success in the hobby. Clubs often host model contests or shows that allow work of all skill levels to be displayed. A benefit of membership is meeting local people who share the same interest, and forming strong friendships centred on enthusiasm for the hobby.

Internet websites have become virtual hobby clubs for a global membership. Questions on many modelling subjects can be asked and answered quickly. Modellers can post photographs of their work in progress or completed, with critique and helpful comments returned from peers. Kits and reference material can be traded, and spare parts located and obtained. These sites also contain links to the many vendors of kits and accessories, so that modellers have access to virtually all products available through online purchase or mail order. Product reviews have been posted on numerous websites allowing the modeller the chance to get a look at parts and accessories before buying them. Some of the most frequented AFV modelling web sites can be found at:

http://missing-lynx.com
http://www.armorama.com
http://www.planetarmor.com
http://www.militarymodelling.com
http://www.track-link.net

Work area and basic tools

Perhaps all modellers start out working from the kitchen table, but a dedicated, properly organized, well-lit area is ideal for model building. Work areas can be split into separate construction and painting spaces if available room allows that luxury. It's handy to keep both modelling tools and reference material within easy reach. A floor with a hard flat surface makes it easier to find those inevitably dropped parts, while an office mat under the model desk is helpful on a carpeted surface.

Small storage drawer cabinets are ideal for keeping spare parts, small subassemblies and other bits and pieces organized and safe. For those that have a difficult time focusing on small parts, magnifiers are available in many forms from inexpensive glasses from the local pharmacy to Opti-Visors, commonly used by jewellers.

The process of trimming, sanding and filing can make a dusty mess, and it's advantageous to have a vacuum system available. Cloths and paper tissue always come in handy for dealing with spills, as even the most careful modellers have had the odd accident with a bottle of paint or glue.

Throughout this book there'll be mention of many tools useful in the construction of AFV models. For anyone new to the hobby, a visit to a local hobby shop will provide most of the essential items needed, and experience will dictate what can be acquired along the way. As mentioned previously, peer groups online and locally can provide information on the available tools, and also any new innovations that have just been introduced to the hobby.

A well-organized area with plenty of room for parts storage, handy references and hobby tools is illustrated in this view of military artist Ron Volstad's modelling area. The innovative idea of a blue cloth can be seen in the seating area, which is placed up on the knees to catch any dropped parts.

Basic construction

Some thoughts to keep in mind when putting together a model kit are the criteria used in judging them in contests. The fit and alignment of all components should be straight, especially the running gear and track runs. All joints on the model should show no seams or gaps that weren't apparent on the real vehicle. The surface of the model should be kept clean from glue marks, fingerprints and other blemishes.

After opening a new kit, it's a good idea to check it for completeness and damage. The shop where the kit was purchased can possibly exchange it if there is a problem, and kit manufacturers are usually quite prompt at replacing missing or damaged parts.

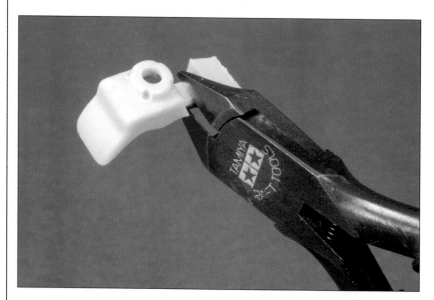

Tamiya's small side-cutters are ideal for removing parts from their pour plugs or styrene runners. Care should be used to cut only plastic, and they should last for years.

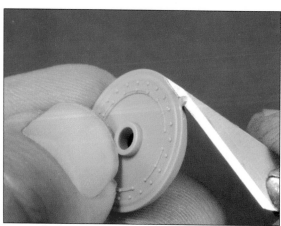

Trimming the burrs and seams on kit parts is handled with a sharp No. 11 hobby blade. To shave the flash from the styrene, a scraping motion works well.

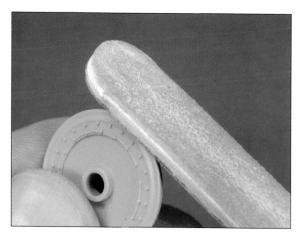

Sanding sticks are available in coarse, medium and fine grades. A medium type is being used to smooth down the seam lines of the Char B1 bis kit wheel.

Some kits, especially those from some of the Eastern European manufacturers, exhibit a fair amount of mould-release agent on the surface of the plastic, and this can cause problems during the painting stages. This greasy residue should be removed by washing the parts when still on the styrene runners in soapy water. Extreme care is needed when doing this, since some of the more delicate pieces can be broken or lost in the washing and drying process.

Plastic kit parts are best separated from their styrene runner run by clipping them with a sharp pair of side-cutters. The flat-sided kind made by Tamiya is ideal for this task, but inexpensive alternatives are available in hardware shops. By cutting the part and leaving a small amount of the sprue tab showing, the tab can be carefully sliced or sanded off without damage to the part itself.

The injection-moulding process occasionally leaves circular depressions on parts. Manufacturers generally take care to ensure that these marks are hidden from view on the finished model by placing them in discrete locations. When these marks appear on the surface of a model that will be displayed, they need to be filled. A small amount of putty and sandpaper usually does the trick, but in the case of deeper marks, it's better to stamp out a disc of styrene sheet, and glue it into the depression. After this has dried, putty can be applied and the surface later sanded smooth to ensure the surface is blemish free.

'Flash' refers to the excess plastic that has seeped between the two halves of the injection moulds and formed a line that needs to be removed. It's rare to see an excess of flash, but mould seams of some degree are always present on the parts and need to be removed. Rather than slice this from the surface, a sharp No. 11 hobby blade should be held perpendicular to the seam and lightly dragged across it. This scraping motion will remove the flash; the same technique can be used to smooth joints on glued seams once dry.

Styrene cement for model kits comes in several forms, but the most common glue used by the AFV modelling community is the thin liquid from a bottle supplied with a small application brush. Cementing styrene parts together should be done with a minimum amount of glue since it's not uncommon to find that parts have been placed in the wrong location. If a part needs to be repositioned, this will allow it to be done with minimum damage.

To stamp out circular pieces of styrene, the punch and die set is a valuable tool. This set from Waldron was used to detail the idler wheels for the Char B1 bis kit.

When small parts are dropped onto the floor, they can be found by scanning the area with a torch (flashlight) from a very low angle with the room light turned off. The light will reflect off anything raised from the surface of the floor, usually revealing the errant part, along with a host of other things best left unmentioned.

The thin cement does have a nasty habit of 'wicking' onto carelessly placed fingers and onto the model's surface. If test-fitting needs a small amount of cement to 'tack' parts together temporarily, it is best to do this using a small amount of cyanoacrylate (Super Glue or Krazy Glue). Small amounts of this glue allows joints to be separated later to help with the building process. Syringe-needle type glue applicators are available to the hobbyist, and allow precise placement and a controlled amount of the liquid on the model. A small piece of stretched kit sprue can also help apply small amounts of crazy glue in hard to reach places.

It's fairly crucial to check the alignment of parts as the glue is setting, which can take the better part of a couple of hours. A glued joint typically needs several hours to cure before it can be sanded smooth.

Joints in the parts, and other areas of the kit such as sink holes, need to be filled with a compound and sanded smooth. For smaller gaps and shallow areas, a lacquer-based tube putty such as Tamiya's Basic Type or Squadron Green Putty can do the job. This compound is applied thinly to the joint and sanded smooth after drying overnight. For larger tasks where some strength is required, two-part epoxy putty is the best choice. The 'A' and 'B' components are kneaded together and pressed into position, and smoothed down with either the same brand thinner or water. This then dries rock-hard overnight, and can be worked on thereafter.

Large joints and holes can also be filled with styrene. Styrene rod of the right diameter, or better yet, the runner from the kit parts, heated and stretched, will form the perfect plug for filling a hole. A styrene wedge can be also cut, dampened with glue, and pushed into stubborn gaps to give them a robust filling.

Special attention should be paid to the alignment of a vehicle's running gear. When constructing a tracked vehicle, the drive sprockets, road wheels, idlers and return rollers should all be straight and sit equidistant from the side of the hull. Kits can suffer from wobbly wheels when the mounts are slightly undersized. They can be beefed up by adding small strips of thin styrene, or deforming them with a pair of pliers to give a tighter fit. A steel ruler can be used to check the alignment of road wheels.

A common feature of some of the latest kits on the market is individual track links or the link-and-length type that provide a more realistic look than the older rubber-band type present on earlier kits. These links are best pieced together in sections of 10 at a time, which helps keep track of their number. The instruction sheet will give an idea of how many are needed for each side, and occasionally a link or two has to be added or removed depending on the sit of the track run and how much 'sag' you want to leave. Thin liquid glue should be dabbed in at each joint, taking care that excess is not added. When piecing together the styrene track run, a steel ruler can help to align the eventual full length when it is cemented together. Once the glue in the track run has had a few minutes to set, it can be wrapped around the running gear and formed around the return rollers. To remove the tracks later for painting, an unglued joint can be left on the drive sprocket, or the running gear can be removed from its mounts by breaking a weak cyanoacrylate bond. Experience has shown that cyanoacrylate does not always want to come apart as easily as one would like, and so caution is advised when using this method.

By making the idler wheels of a model adjustable, the track links can be more accurately portrayed, especially in the case of the workable type of after-

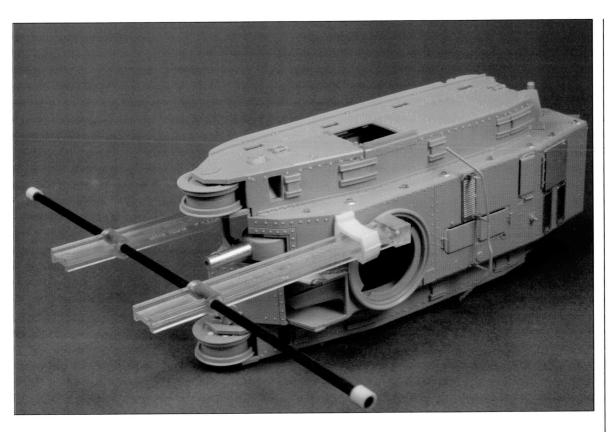

market tracks. By changing the position of the idler wheel, the correct tension can be set on the track run depending on the number of track links used on the kit. Some kits provide this feature, but for those that need to add it, the mount for the idler wheel can be given a snug fit by squeezing the mount with pliers until it deforms to fit snugly enough to stay in place, while allowing a small amount of adjustment.

When constructing the model's hull, it can be helpful to tape together the larger sections, holding them into place while the glue sets. Caution must be exercised to ensure that liquid glue does not get underneath the sections of tape and ruin the kit's surface. An additional method of holding the hull sections is to use large hobby clamps. If the sides of the hull tend to warp inwards, particularly in the middle, they can be braced by cementing a length of .125 × .250in. styrene bar between the walls.

Most of the vehicle tools can be glued onto the kit, rather than painting them and adding them later. If crew figures will be in the vehicle, they can be temporarily located and the hatches glued in position.

As the upper hull of the model begins to take shape, some of the additional parts such as mounted figures and stowage should be test fitted. There is nothing worse than finding out that some well-posed tank riders won't fit the model because of an interfering hatch, antenna or other obstruction that wasn't picked up until too late.

The painting process will be dealt with later in the book, but consideration should be given during construction to any parts that should be painted before the final stages of kit assembly. It is advantageous to paint the interior of a model flat black in case it can be seen through crew hatches or other such openings. If the vehicle features any interior detail, then this would of course need to be finished beforehand.

Hobby clamps can be used to hold larger sections of a model in place during assembly. Stubborn pieces that want to spring apart can also be restrained with tape.

Advanced construction and techniques

After-market accessories

Once the basics of AFV model construction have been mastered, it follows that the hobbyist will want to strive for improvements in accuracy and detail. There is also a drive to want to create something unique from the mainstream of kit assembly, for instance to modify or convert a model from how it is presented in the box. After-market modelling items are produced to satisfy this requirement, and have been around since the beginning of the hobby. At first rather crude, they have become well researched and finely produced in recent years. Because of the limitations placed on injection-moulded styrene parts, some kit detail is often sacrificed to produce a reasonable facsimile of the subject. Because most after-market accessory parts are produced in resin castings and photo-etched brass, there is almost no limit to the intricacy of detail that can now be provided.

One of the frustrations of researching a modelling subject is the discovery that some kits have notable inaccuracies. The after-market industry provides many fixes, typically in the form of newly designed resin parts that are sized to fit the particular kit in question. Instruction sheets included can be sometimes rather sketchy, and references are certainly a help when adding the details.

Track links

Improving the look of the track runs was always a problem until the after-market industry produced individual link tracks. The previous vinyl track runs made models look quite toy-like if placed on AFV models that featured sagging links between the return rollers on the real thing. Sometimes costing more

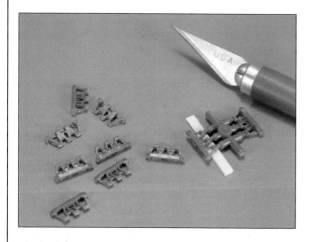

The Cromwell Panzerbefehlswagen III kit includes a set of link and length resin tracks that were discarded in favour of a more detailed set of Modelkasten SK-57 workable styrene tracks. The guide teeth on the actual track links were taller than either the kit tracks or the Modelkasten set, so using either would have been a compromise on the overall accuracy of the model. The Modelkasten links were removed from their carrier sprue using a new hobby knife blade with a piece of styrene strip backing to support the link during the cut to avoid damaging it.

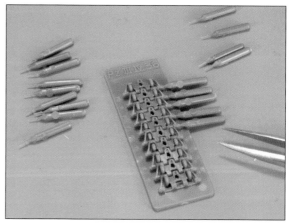

The Modelkasten tracks are provided with a jig to align ten links to receive the individual track pins. The outer end of the pins has an S-shaped cotter pin moulded on while the inside end has a flat head so it is important to ensure that the ends do not get mixed up. A small dab of Testor's Liquid Cement was applied with an old paintbrush to each pin before inserting it into the hole in the link.

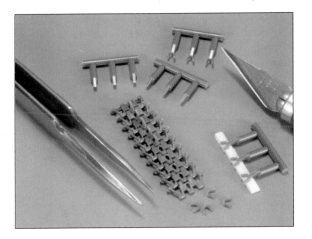

The small seams on each side of the guide teeth were removed with the tip of a hobby knife and then cut from the carrier sprue. They were then glued to the links and, after they were sufficiently dry, the cut edges were sanded smooth.

The tracks were fitted to the hull before proceeding with the rest of the construction. The idler axles are not movable and this resulted in a slightly loose track on the right side of the model. Removing one link had the opposite effect in that the track was then too tight.

money than the kit itself, individual track links have added a significant dimension of realism to AFV modelling. Several companies produce styrene, resin and white metal alloy workable types of links.

Modelkasten from Japan have an extensive line of specialized track links. The styrene track sets are very finely moulded and are assembled by gluing pins into each side of the individual links, allowing them to swivel like the real thing. Some sets are quite elaborate, and can consist of many individual parts per link to allow significant detail to be reproduced. One disadvantage of these sets is that they tend to be more delicate than other brands of track links, and care has to be taken when painting, weathering and handling the completed runs.

The Hungarian company Friulmodel is a manufacturer of white-metal tracks and other detailed parts that are extremely well researched. Their wide range of track link types cover subjects from pre-World War II to the modern day. These

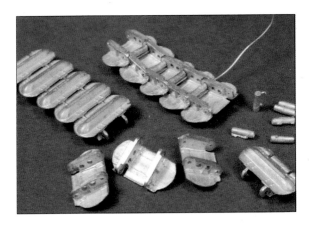

Friulmodel offers a large range of after-market track links made from white metal. These links for the Char B1 bis kit are wired together. Because of the nature of how the links are moulded, a fair amount of clean-up is needed with a sharp hobby blade and a small file.

The difference between the kit tracks (in brown styrene) and the Friulmodel tracks with regard to shape and detail can be seen in this view of the model.

tracks must be cleaned up by trimming small amounts of metal 'flash' from each link, including the track pin holes. The links are fastened together using a supplied soft wire, with care being taken to not stab one's own finger when poking it through each link, then securing it with a drop of cyanoacrylate.

World War II Productions from Australia make resin track links that snap together by flexing each link onto the pins in each adjacent one. Although the production is of a limited range, the shape and detail of these links is superb.

Some of the mainstream manufacturers such as Tamiya and AFV Club have produced separately packaged individual track links, and DML currently provide what they refer to as 'Magic Tracks' with their kits, which are individual links that require no separation or clean-up from a sprue. These styrene links glue together, similarly to the Modelkasten non-workable kind, and require a bit more effort to get the required look compared with the workable kind that basically falls into place.

Vehicle interiors

Resin detail manufacturers offer many interior sets for plastic kits. These elaborate sets are kits in themselves, and may also include photo-etched brass and various other pieces. Adding the interior parts often involves modifying the inside of the model's hull by removing supports and thinning down other surfaces to ensure a correct fit.

Testing the fit of interior parts during assembly is essential if serious problems are to be avoided later. There is nothing worse than discovering that the two halves of the hull will not mate because of a completely constructed and painted interior that is too large. Alignment of parts should also be considered, and continually checked as assembly progresses. For instance, the gun sight of the Sturmgeschütz III self-propelled gun has to be able to end up positioned in a hole in the roof and also be located properly on the main gun. Owing to the thickness of the model's hull, there usually is not the same amount of scale room inside the kit to lay out properly all of the details as they appear in references of the real vehicle, and some compromises are inevitable.

Using photo references, some of the wiring and cabling can be added to the interior using fine copper wire and thin solder wire. To add strength to the joints where the wires hook up, it's wise to drill a small hole and glue the wire in place. This is especially handy when wiring a vehicle radio set, and there is some stress placed on the joints when moving and positioning the components into place.

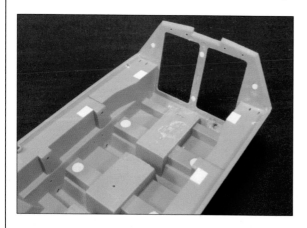

The hull for the LAV-25 model was prepared for interior detail. Discs and strips of sheet styrene are glued in place to fill in moulding marks. The styrene is sanded down and imperfections filled with Tamiya grey putty.

Occasionally the moulding of the kit will interfere with interior builds. Here a support bulkhead needs to be cut away to resemble the actual interior. Ejector-pin marks and rough spots have been filled with Tamiya putty and await sanding.

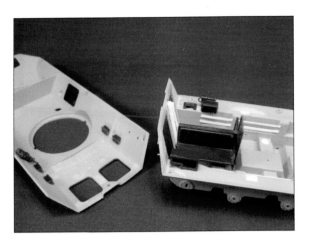

Spare interior parts from the Italeri LAV-25 and some additional styrene detail provide an adequate base for the interior. Fuel fill pipes between the rear doors are made from Evergreen tubing.

The finished interior. Resin ammunition boxes, lead foil seat belts and placard decals help to fill up empty spaces and provide interest. As the rear doors will be closed, and the figures will be filling up most of the upper hatches, additional detail is not really necessary.

Brass detail

Photo-etched brass parts have offered the world of AFV modelling a new dimension in intricate detail that was hard to achieve with styrene or resin parts. Brass fenders, workable tool clamps and even tiny pairs of spectacles for figures are just some examples of what is available, allowing the modeller more options to create realism in their work.

Typically produced on brass runners, the photo-etched parts can be removed using a sharp No. 11 hobby blade against a hard flat surface, such as a piece of glass or a ceramic tile. Cutting it on a plastic cutting board may distort the part. Etched-metal scissors are also available, but are not recommended for this purpose since they are difficult to insert into the crowded runners in most cases. The edge of the cut should be smoothed off carefully with a sanding stick or file, ensuring that the strokes are parallel with the edge of the brass and not across, which would bend it. Holding the brass near the edge with a good pair of tweezers or flat-nosed pliers also helps the process.

To trim etched-metal parts from their runners, a sharp blade should be used against a hard flat surface such as a ceramic tile, or as in this case, a piece of glass. The cut should be made as close as possible to the part, and the edge filed carefully afterwards.

This photo demonstrates how moveable steering can be obtained using the photo-etched parts in conjunction with the modified kit pieces. The styrene rod has been drilled out to allow fine-tuning of the steering radius.

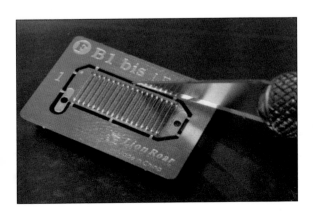

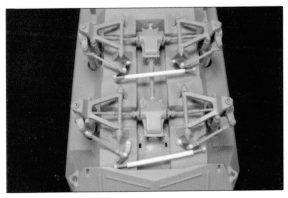

Etched-metal numbers from the Lion Roar detail set for the Char B1 bis were glued in place with cyanoacrylate. The styrene on the outside of the support is a spacer added for proper fit on the model.

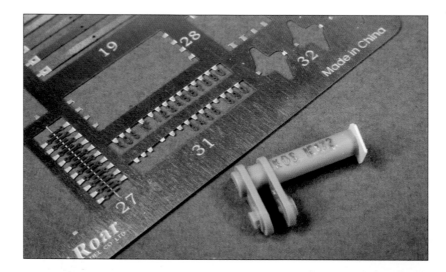

Brass fender sections from the Lion Roar detail set were added to Tamiya's Char B1 bis kit by bending the parts with a Hold and Fold tool, and soldering the mounts to the lower sides.

Tamiya's German bicycle kit was detailed with Aber's etched-brass set. The plastic spokes were carved out to accommodate the delicate brass replacements, lining them up with the filaments from an ink eraser brush.

The detail of the bicycle model was enhanced by adding some stowage on the rear carrier using items from some DML figure sets, and strapping them down with lead sheet strips. A folded ground sheet was made from epoxy putty.

Bending the smaller brass parts can be done using some of the commercially available tools such as the Etch-Mate or Hold and Fold, or by using some flat-ended pliers or tweezers. The commercial tools are invaluable for making straight bends, especially in the case of larger sections of brass such as fender sections and replacement hull walls.

Cementing brass parts to a model or to each other is a rather tricky process, since cyanoacrylate is rather fast to set and the parts are small, hard to manipulate and very delicate. It is advisable to use a small amount of styrene glue to tack the part into place initially, and then add cyanoacrylate to make a permanent bond when it is properly positioned. The brass part can also be initially glued to a thin styrene base using .005in. styrene card, and then easily mounted in place with styrene cement. Brass parts can be cemented to each other using cyanoacrylate, with a slower setting time providing the modeller extra time for correct positioning.

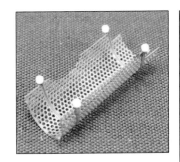

After the screening for the LAV-25 model was formed (by rolling it gently back and forth on a soft eraser with an appropriately sized tube of brass), small disks of styrene were glued to the mounts. This way it was easier to fit and adjust with plastic cement.

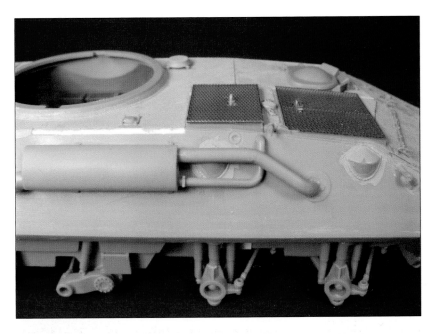

The moulded screening around the exhaust pipe was replaced with the Voyager photo-etched pieces. Here a section of the kit sprue is used to make the exhaust piping to the muffler. Weld beads have been added around the shock tower cones, and photo-etched screens have been added to the engine grilles.

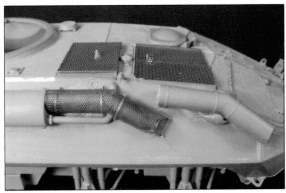

The kit exhaust guard on the right, showing the detail improvement provided by the photo-etched parts and (unfortunately barely visible) exhaust pipe.

Additional details added for the LAV-25 System Life Extension Program (SLEP) vehicles seen in Iraq include the driver's external display mounted on the back of the periscope cluster. This was fabricated from strip styrene and a small piece of lead wire. Also visible is the anti-slip texture simulated by stippling Mr Surfacer 500 on the upper surfaces.

Some brass joints need added strength, such as those on fenders or stowage bins that will be bent to simulate damage. In these cases it is best to solder the parts together. To prepare the parts for soldering, they should be free from any grease and be given a preparatory scrubbing with sandpaper or a glass fibre pen. After treating both surfaces to a light coating of flux paste, the parts should be positioned together with copper clips. Small pieces of solder wire can then be sliced from a length and placed around the joints. By heating the joints with a soldering tool, the solder will melt wicking itself into the fluxed joint after which the heat can be removed. An electric soldering pen will work for this, although better results can be obtained using a miniature butane torch. To protect any adjacent solder joints on the brass part a heat sink can be positioned in the form of wet tissue paper or a flat copper clip. After soldering the parts, the excess flux and grease can be removed using a vinegar wash.

Working with resin parts

Most commercially available detail accessories for kit modification are urethane resin castings. These parts are generally extremely well detailed since they come from soft rubber moulds, unlike the styrene parts that suffer from the limitations of the injection-moulding process. The resin material is softer than styrene and easier to cut and sand, and can be adhered with cyanoacrylate or two-part epoxy glue. Occasionally it may help to attach resin parts to a thin styrene base using cyanoacrylate, and then use the base along with styrene cement to position the part. This method does allow for some extra handling time.

Occasionally resin update parts are poorly cast with disfiguring air bubbles. The kit part was modified with styrene strip and bolt heads, and had the top edge thinned down with a hobby blade using the resin part as a guide.

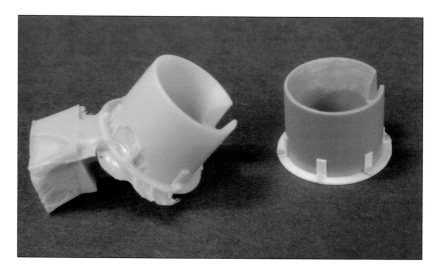

The castings can be removed from their pour plugs using a thin razor saw blade. Pour plugs can occasionally be large in size, in which case they can be nibbled down with a pair of sharp side-cutters before making the final cut. Larger resin castings that have wide areas of excess to remove can be placed on a piece of sandpaper and ground down using a circular motion. This can generate a fair bit of resin dust, and caution should be exercised to not inhale the particles.

Resin castings can contain air bubbles that can weaken the part or cause a disfigurement not easily seen until the painting stages of the project. These cavities should be filled with small amounts of epoxy putty when discovered.

Warped parts are commonly found with resin castings, and these can usually be straightened by immersing them in hot water. The part can then be bent back into place while hot, and then cooled quickly while being held straight. A poorly formed part occasionally has to be remade in styrene using the original resin part as a guide.

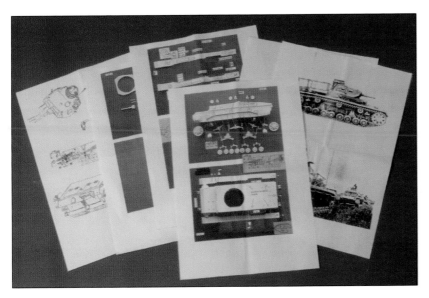

The instruction sheets that accompany cottage industry resin kits are generally less detailed than those found in mainstream plastic model kits, and this further underscores the need for additional reference material.

The flexible rubber moulds used to cast resin kits allow the manufacturers to produce more complex shapes in one piece resulting in fewer parts to assemble.

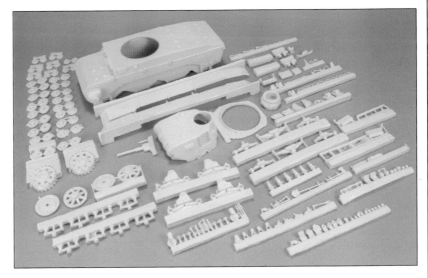

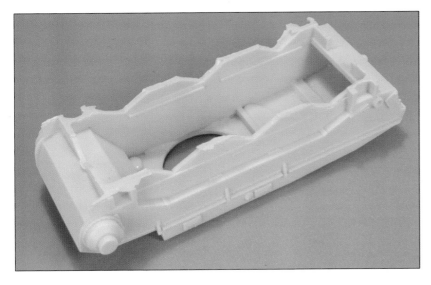

The one-piece hull casting for the Cromwell Panzerbefehlswagen III had several large pour blocks located along the bottom edge that required careful removal with a razor saw and sanding in order to avoid damaging the part..

23

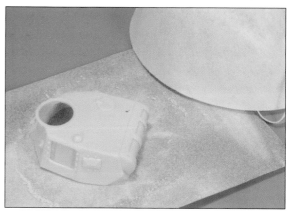

The complex drive sprockets were cast in one piece and featured very fine detail. A small amount of flash was present inside the holes in the outer face, which was easily removed with the tip of a hobby knife.

The pour block on the bottom of the turret shell was removed by sanding in a circular fashion on a piece of sandpaper. After five rotations, the position of the turret in my hand was changed so that the pressure was evenly distributed and was constantly checked to ensure that it was not over-sanded. Since resin dust can be a health hazard, it is advisable to use a mask to avoid breathing in the dust.

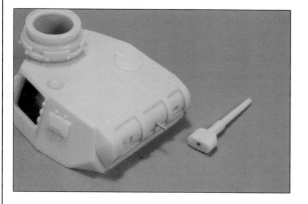

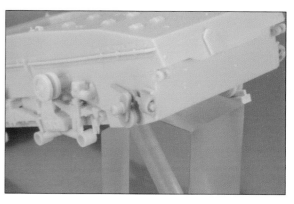

The back of the dummy 3.7cm gun barrel was sanded with a piece of sandpaper wrapped around a .375in.-diameter styrene tube to mate properly with the front of the mantlet and secured in place with a short piece of .040in. diameter aluminium rod.

The rear idler adjusting mechanism was not provided with the resin kit and came from my spares box. Since the most current references are not clear on this detail, some degree of licence was taken in the decision to use them. The idler axles are also from the spares box and were used primarily as the resin parts had some small air bubbles that would have been difficult to repair.

A jig to keep the road wheels properly aligned was made from .040 × .080in. and .100 × .188in. Evergreen styrene strip.

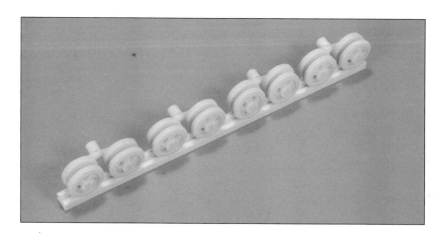

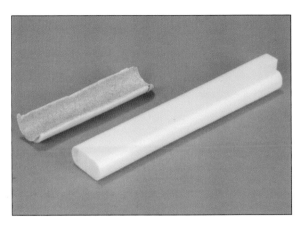

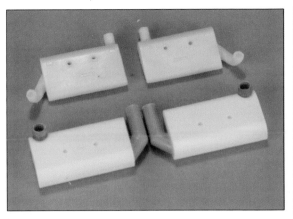

Newer references provided information that the mufflers were actually larger rectangular shapes with rounded top and bottom edges. Two .188 × .188in. Evergreen styrene strips were laminated together to obtain the basic shape and the edges were rounded using sandpaper glued to the inside of a piece of .375in. diameter styrene tube.

The exhaust pipes leading into and out of the mufflers were made from pieces of sprue. The kit mufflers are shown above the new mufflers for comparison.

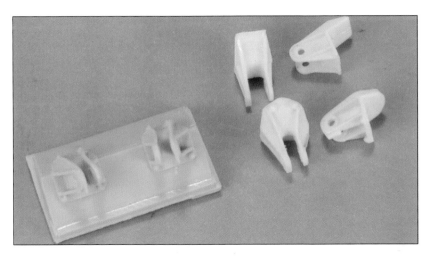

The front tow shackles were replaced with resin versions cast from a master that I made several years ago and are more accurate than the kit parts. The kit parts, copied from the DML Panzerkampfwagen III Ausf. G, are shown above for comparison.

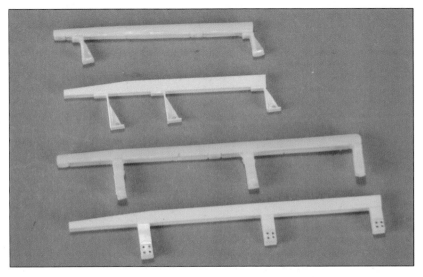

The resin antenna troughs provided with the kit are a bit inaccurate, had a few air bubbles and were replaced with others made from various sizes of Evergreen styrene strip.

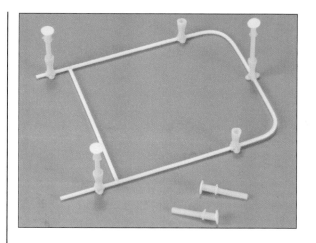

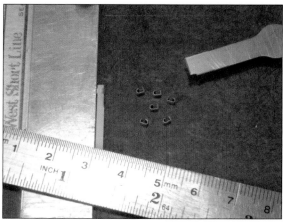

Only the five supports for the frame antenna were provided with the kit. The antenna was made using a piece of .030in.-diameter styrene rod that was bent to shape around the handle of a hobby knife. The supports were drilled out and the styrene rod threaded through them. The two in front and the back one were glued in place and the assembly glued to the engine deck. The two centre supports were then trimmed to fit so they wouldn't distort the shape of the antenna.

The tow cable stowage brackets were made from leftover photo-etched brass frets shaped over a piece of styrene strip. After making one, it was flattened out and measured for length so all of them would be identical.

Wherever possible, the kit tools were replaced with others taken from the DML Panzerkampfwagen III Ausf. J kit as they are more accurately detailed. The engine crank handle had to be cut apart on each side of the brackets and glued back together to obtain the correct orientation. The scratch-built antenna trough has been glued in place.

The unusual method of stowing the tow cable can be seen here along with the brass rod replacement engine deck hatch handles. Some of these vehicles were fitted with a folding step on the side and this one was taken from the Aber photo-etched brass detail set for a Panzer IV.

The two machine-gun barrels in the mantlet were spares from a DML set and the two rod antennae were from the DML Panzerkampfwagen III Ausf. J kit.

Casting your own resin parts

Casting resin parts is a method of duplicating an existing part. This is a handy way to make several copies of a scratch-built item that may be otherwise quite labour intensive, or to provide a second necessary kit part preventing the need to pilfer one from an otherwise complete kit.

An RTV rubber mould first needs to be made of the original part. If the part is a simple item that can be made with a flat back, then it can be mounted on a flat surface and have four walls formed around it high enough to cover it to the top. The walls can typically be made from styrene or even blocks of Lego bricks. After placing the object within the walls, the surface of it and the inside of the walls should be lightly coated in a mould-release agent. A dab of Vaseline grease with an old paintbrush usually does the trick. The RTV rubber is prepared by adding a measured amount of coloured catalyst, and stirring until the mixture

In order to place the model in a historical context on a scenic base, a French road sign was scratch-built from a resin casting, styrene strip and dry transfer lettering. A photo from a book was used as a guide.

Using a printed road sign from a *Steel Masters* magazine as a guide for the size of the lettering, the sign was made with Woodland Scenics' dry transfer letters on a printed blue background. The name of the department and the highway number were made on a printed red background. The final size of the sign was determined by the size of the lettered background.

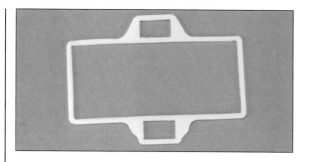

The shape of the sign was drawn onto a piece of .020in. styrene sheet and carefully cut out with a hobby knife.

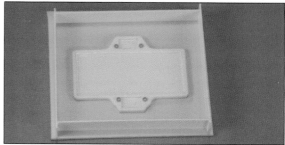

The frame was glued to a piece of .030in. styrene sheet which was then trimmed to the same size as the frame. A .015 × .015in. styrene strip was added to the inside edge of the frame and additional detail scribed into and glued onto the sign following the photo from the book. The finished piece was glued to a .040in. styrene sheet and bordered with a .020 × .250in. styrene strip to form a dam for the rubber.

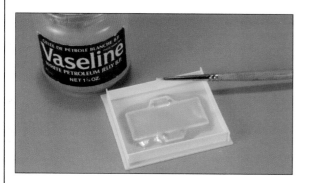

Petroleum jelly was lightly brushed into the mould to act as a release agent and a thin film of the casting rubber was brushed on to eliminate any air bubbles that might form against the part master.

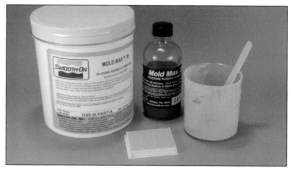

Smooth-On Mold Max 30 is a two-part room temperature vulcanizing rubber used in making moulds for resin casting. One part of the catalyst in the red bottle was added to ten parts of the rubber and thoroughly mixed together in a liquid laundry detergent-measuring cup using a disposable wooden stir stick.

LEFT After curing overnight, the rubber mould was removed from the master.

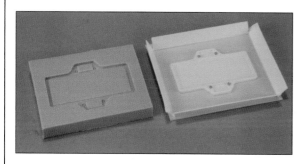

RIGHT Smooth-On Smooth-Cast 300 White Liquid Plastic was used to produce a resin casting of the sign. Two equal parts of each component were measured into disposable film canisters with pipettes, and were then quickly and thoroughly mixed together. The mixture was gently poured into the rubber mould and the air bubbles removed with a straight pin. There are only a few minutes of working time before the resin begins to harden so the process must be done quickly. After removing the casting from the rubber mould, the back was sanded flat and the pedestal base added from styrene strip.

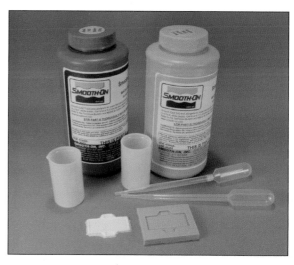

The tow cable was painted with Humbrol HS217 Steel enamel paint and given a heavy wash of black artist's oil paint. A light coat of Tamiya X-25 Clear Green acrylic paint was brushed onto the glass vision block on the turret side hatch to produce a greenish tinge.

looks homogeneous. The rubber, in liquid form, can be painted onto the part to be copied to ensure a good coating with no bubbles, and the remainder poured into the small enclosure. After several hours of curing time, the rubber mould will have set, and the original part can then be carefully extracted.

To make a copy, two-part urethane resin is mixed in equal amounts and then poured into the rubber mould. Using a toothpick, small pockets of air that get trapped in the small crevices can be moved out ensuring that the mould gets completely filled with resin. Depending on the type of resin, the duplicate part will be hardened and ready to pop out of the mould within five to ten minutes. Release agent must be added to the moulds before pouring the resin to help the separation of the resin part or else damage to the mould can result.

More complicated parts can be duplicated using a two-sided mould. For this, the part is pressed halfway into a clay-like surface such as plasticine before forming the first half of the mould. The process described above is carried out to make the first half of the mould. Once this has cured, the plasticine is removed and the part is placed into the rubber. Walls are again formed around the first half of the mould, the surfaces are coated with release agent, and the second half of the mould is poured onto it. To make the duplicate part is a little trickier than the simple single pour method, since resin must be added to each

The turrets on the Panzerbefehlswagen III Ausf. D1, Ausf. E and Ausf. H were bolted to the hull. This allowed for the unusual placement of the Balkenkreuz on the side of the vehicles utilized by 2.Panzer-Division during the Blitzkrieg era.

The mufflers were weathered with various rusty coloured pastel chalks from the Rembrandt line. The wooden supports for the frame antenna on the engine deck were painted with Humbrol 160 German Camouflage Red Brown and given a wash of Designer's Gouache burnt umber watercolour paint to give them the appearance of wood.

half of the mould. The two halves are brought together just before the material cures, forming the complete part within the cavity. This somewhat primitive method can produce some good results if the two mould halves line up correctly, and the resin doesn't trap any air bubbles. Several attempts can sometimes be necessary to make the required part adequately.

Scratch-building

One of the most difficult but rewarding sets of techniques used in the hobby of AFV modelling is scratch-building. The term is used loosely to describe the construction of part of an AFV model from components built by the modeller himself, typically using styrene sheet. It's unusual for a modeller to scratch-build an entire vehicle from handmade parts, since wheels, gun barrels, tracks and other elements of the build are usually purchased items. Scratch-built kits are quite an ambitious endeavour and require precise drawings and photographic reference as a guide. Major kit conversions and one-of-a-kind subjects are usually the target of the AFV scratch-builder. The two projects that demonstrate significant scratch-building effort in this title are Steven van Beveren's Jagdpanther which was a conversion based on a Panther Ausf. G kit, and Graeme Davidson's Canadian missile launcher TUA, which was a converted Academy M981 kit.

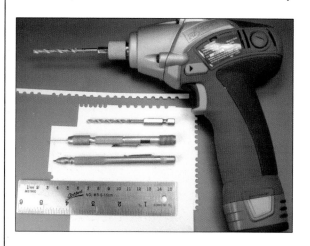

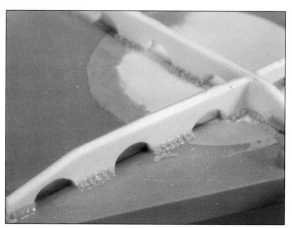

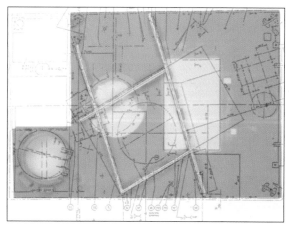

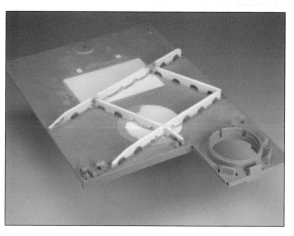

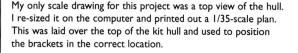

My only scale drawing for this project was a top view of the hull. I re-sized it on the computer and printed out a 1/35-scale plan. This was laid over the top of the kit hull and used to position the brackets in the correct location.

Getting these brackets correct was important, as their location would drive the positioning of all the other modifications to the upper hull.

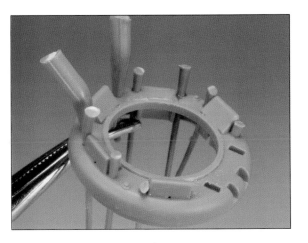

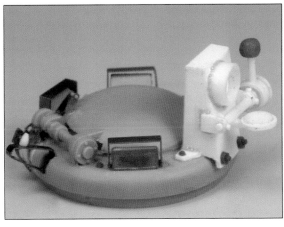

Preparing the commander's cupola for the new sighting unit meant filling in the kit holes. I find stretched sprue plugs work well. These are glued in with a twisting motion and then flush cut when dry.

The commander was equipped with an independent sight that replaced the front episcope. Eduard etch was used for the scope guards and hatch details. A pinch of two-part putty was rolled into a sphere-like shape for the handle grip; however, this was later replaced by some steel shot.

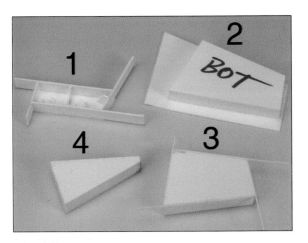

This shows my sequence for making the hull stowage bins. At the top left, an accurate bottom for the bin has been cut, with each side cut long and allowed to overlap. These were braced from the inside using right-angle scraps. Moving clockwise, an oversize top has been roughly cut and glued on. The next bin shows the top trimmed back, and thin strips for the bin lid have been cut oversize. The last bin shows the strips flush cut. Bins like this are the essence of starting in scratch-building – if you have not tried it, you will be amazed at how easy it becomes.

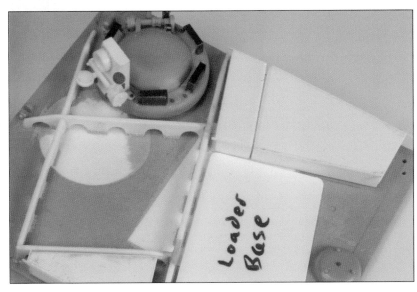

The scale plans paid dividends when it came to sizing and placing the bins on the hull.

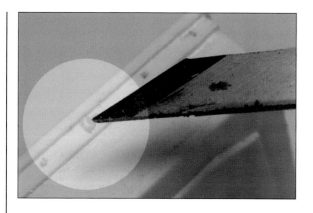

The hinge plate and lid lip of each bin were made using .010 x.060in. and .010 x.020in. strips. Rivets from a sub-miniature punch and die set, and are positioned using a moistened knife edge. I use a bit of spit on the blade, though I can't in good conscience recommend licking your new No. 11 blade as a safe practice!

Locating pins are drilled through the hull roof, and used to align the bins. This allowed me to remove them for painting later on.

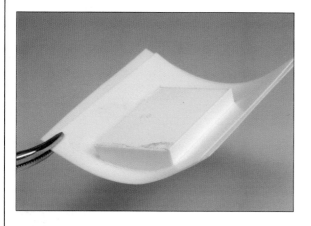

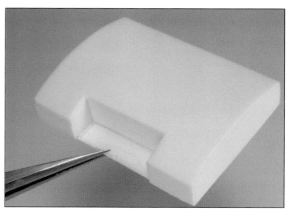

Construction of the loader's hatch begins by laminating two sheets of .005in. to a curved cross section.

The oversize roof is trimmed back and sanded flush.

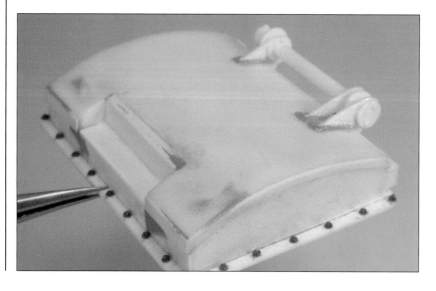

The long, spring-loaded hinge and mounting plate are added, along with some Tichy bolt heads on the mounting plate.

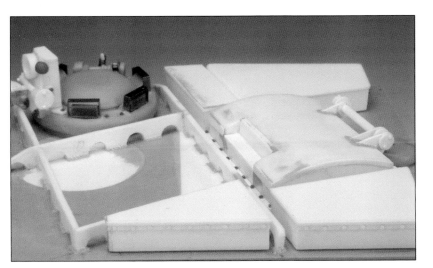

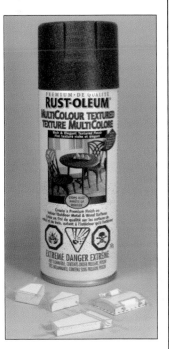

RIGHT This product is marketed under the Rust-oleum name in North America, and can be found at the DIY shop. The parts to be painted are attached to some scrap cardboard with double-sided tape otherwise the force of the spray will blow them around.

The driver's side sprocket mount has a large gap in the hull sponsons. Some oversize sheet stock bridges the gap and provides a gluing surface for an exact cut panel glued from underneath.

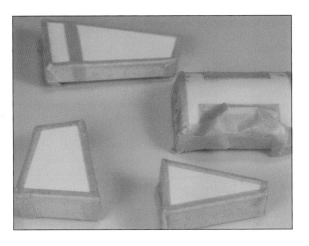

Some of the horizontal surfaces have an anti-slip coating added. The pattern varies from vehicle to vehicle; some have it painted on, others use strips of black grip tape. In preparation for the coating, the parts are masked off.

The Diehl individual link tracks from HKCW are the same as those offered by AFV Club and went together well. M113s with proper track tension have a finger-width gap between the bottom of the track and the top of the third road wheel. Note that the stowage bins have different heights.

After drying for a few minutes, the tape can be removed. Be careful not to touch the surface for an hour or so until the paint has dried.

The front hull has all the holes filled using scrap styrene in preparation for the photo-etch parts.

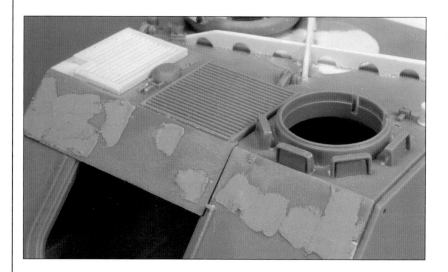

These are cut flush and puttied over.

Maple Leaf Models' external fuel tanks and fuel can brackets were used. Note that these have the correct double-angled bottom – the kit ones are curved. The MLM external fuel tanks come with Canadian-pattern brake lights and housings.

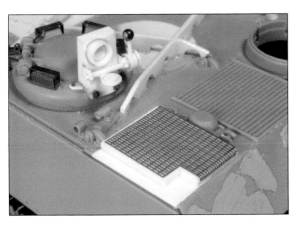

The Academy engine deck has the exhaust port in the wrong location for a Canadian M113, so a new vent grille was made from strip stock, and the Eduard etch screen was notched to fit. The hand-rolled blob used as a handle for the sight cover lever was replaced with some No. 9 steel shot.

Work on the turret began with the base. The approach to this was rather unsophisticated – a circle template and scissors was used to cut a series of discs.

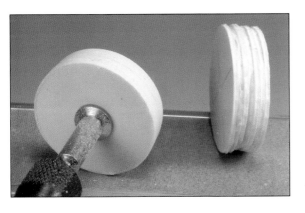

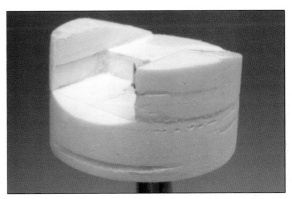

These were laminated, clamped and set aside to dry. They were then chucked in a Dremel and turned at low speed against a sanding block.

This yielded three squat cylinders, which were cut and notched to accept the turret sighting module and main body.

The fire-control module houses the optical and thermal sights and a laser rangefinder. This unit was made in the same manner as the turret base.

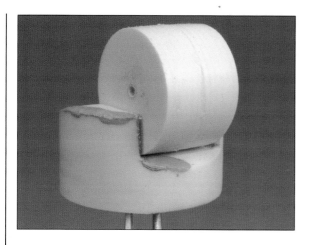

The base unit and fire-control module after sanding. The base was skimmed with a thin sheet of styrene.

Test fitting throughout the construction process is important, especially when you do not have scale plans. Here the turret is mocked up to make sure it can freely rotate, and that it does not interfere with the commander's cupola.

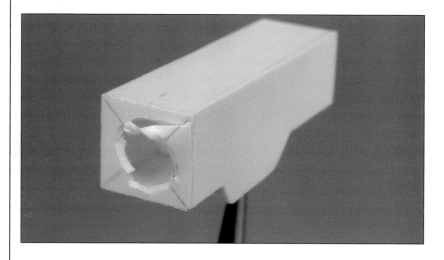

I set the turret aside to work on the missile launchers. I found it quite difficult to get a dead-on centred hole on the face of the launcher. Using a drill bit that matched the final diameter hole yielded a somewhat rough edge. Scratch one launcher.

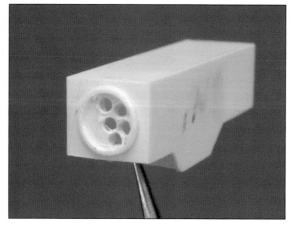

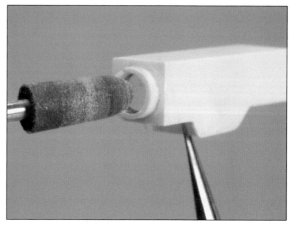

I found that a thinly sliced ring of tube stock was easy to centre on the face of the launcher. Once glued in place, it was just a matter of cutting out the middle part ...

... and then using a conical sanding bit to smooth out the edges.

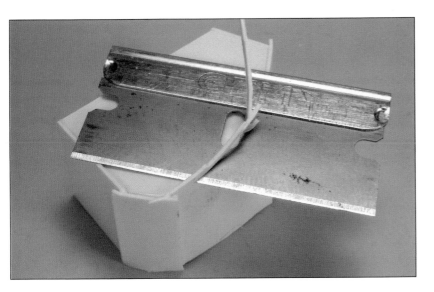

The turret body is really not much more than a box with six sides. As with the stowage bins, the turret sides are cut oversize and trimmed back with a razor.

The main turret components. TOW missile tubes from Italeri's LAV-TUA interior were used to fill out the launcher.

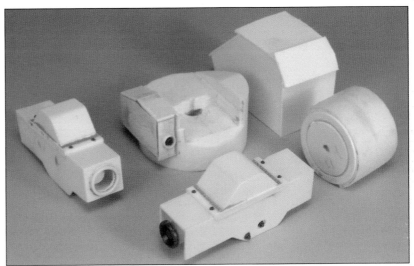

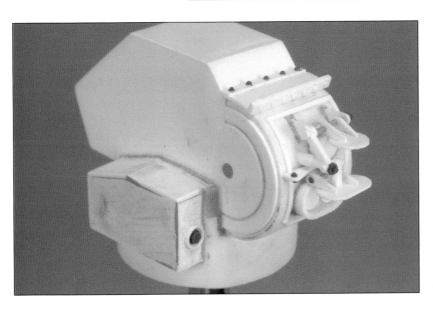

The sight lenses and sight cover mechanism were added to the turret face.

The TUA has a unique routing for engine and heater exhausts to minimize heat shimmer through the various sighting systems. These were made with strip sand rod stock, and then given a rusty texture using Mr Surfacer putty stippled with liquid cement and an old brush.

The engine exhaust pipe was covered with a perforated heat shield.

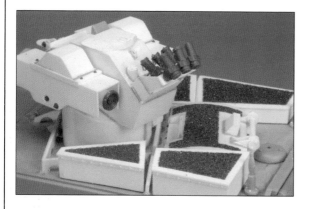

Two banks of three smoke grenades were added to the turret. These came from a Tamiya Leopard and were detailed with Aber photo-etch chains.

The lower hull was detailed with reinforcing strips on the final drive housing and a pair of tow shackles from the DML Abrams.

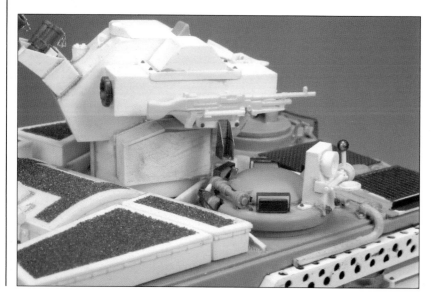

Some final details before painting included etched headlight guards, sheet brass turn-signal housing, MLM spare road wheel and track grouser racks.

A wide range of styrene sheet in various thicknesses is required for this type of work. A good stock of styrene rod and strip also comes in handy, along with a selection of sizes of nuts, bolts and rivet heads. Spare parts from previous modelling builds, and occasionally parts 'borrowed' from an unbuilt model kit, are invaluable when gathering the components needed for a scratch-built project.

Some of the tools necessary for a scratch-building project include a metal straight edge, a protractor for measuring angles, a Chopper tool for making multiple, precise, identical cuts, and a scriber or dental pick to engrave lines in plastic. A set of miniature drill bits and a punch and die set are handy items for making precise holes. Also essential for the task are cutting pads that come with a printed crosshatch; these help to keep angles straight when working.

Technical drawings and plans are important to create the parts needed for the project. Though it should also be kept in mind that the dimensions of a kit used in the build may not match reference drawings, and therefore a significant amount of test fitting, modification and compromise is necessary to help the construction along. Measurements can be roughed out using paper templates initially in order not to waste valuable styrene card. Dimensions can be transferred to styrene sheet by photocopying the reference to the desired scale, transferring it to tracing paper, and marking it through to the styrene sheet with pin pricks.

The styrene card used for making components of the model must be of a sufficient thickness to accept liquid glue without distorting. The white styrene stock is typically much softer than the material used for injection-moulded kits, and a lot less tolerant to cement. If very thin card is required, then cyanoacrylate may be a better choice. The strength and sturdiness of the component created should also be considered when deciding how thick a styrene sheet to use.

The type of joint required needs to be pre-planned when styrene sections are butted together. Armour plates on AFVs had a certain pattern to their assembly, and this can either be emulated in how the panels are glued together, or scribed in later after the sides have been joined. Thought should be given to the angle at which the edges of the styrene sections are cut, keeping the blade poised at the correct slant when running it along the straight-edge. Since there is a slight distortion to the edge of the plastic when a hobby blade makes a lengthwise cut, the raised lip formed needs to be sanded down. Styrene sections can be temporarily fastened together with tape when testing the fit.

Detailing a scratch-built project requires bolt heads, rivets, brass detail and other resin and styrene parts. Hinges for access hatches and doors can come from scrap parts, or be cast from resin using a rubber

Using the DML Panther G Smart Kit as a starting point, Steve van Beveren built up the basic hull shape of the Jagdpanther using sheet styrene.

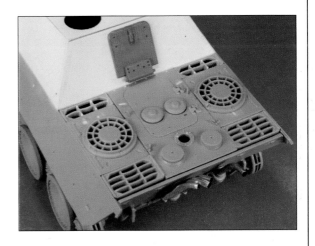

Larger diameter engine deck grilles from a DML Panther A kit were used instead of the Smart Kit's smaller Ausf. G grilles.

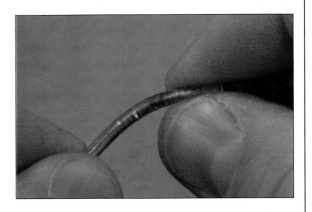

The vehicle's exhaust pipes were made by soldering thin-gauge copper sheet into a tube. To stop the tube from collapsing while bending, a piece of lawn trimmer cord was inserted into it.

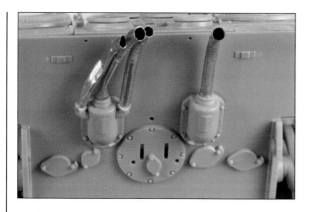

Once bent to the correct shape the lawn trimmer cord was simply pulled from the tube. The exhaust tubes were then mounted to exhaust castings from a DML Panther A kit.

The early Jagdpanthers built by Miag were manufactured with a unique cast bump stop mounted above the first road wheel torsion arm. This was represented by modifying the kit part to resemble this unique casting.

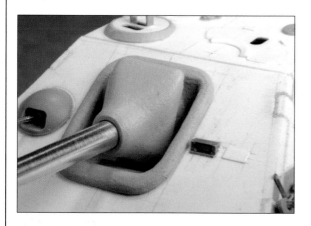

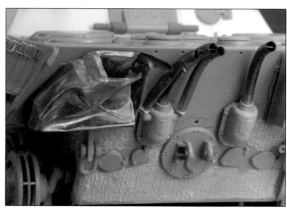

An externally bolted gun recess casting from a Tamiya Jagdpanther kit was re-shaped to represent an early, internally bolted casting.

The left-hand exhaust pipes and stowage bin were damaged to match closely the damage on the Imperial War Museum's Jagdpanther.

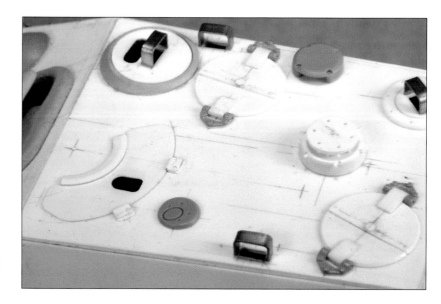

The items on the roof plate were scratch-built from sheet styrene and brass with a few pieces taken from Tamiya and DML kits.

Owing to the damaged exhaust pipes the vehicle jack would no longer fit into its mounting brackets so it was placed on the engine deck.

The spare aerial and gun cleaning rod cylindrical stowage tube end caps were made by embossing thin aluminium sheet over a custom-made styrene master.

The tow cables were made using leftover electrical grounding wire from a ceiling lamp and plastic ends from the DML Panther G kit.

The right-hand front fender was also modified to match the damage visible in period photos of the vehicle taken after its capture by the British.

Rain guards around the various items on the superstructure roof were made using thin gauge copper sheet cut into strips and glued into place using thin cyanoacrylate.

mould. Again, the importance of test fitting during the entire process cannot be overemphasized.

Scratch-building interior components is a challenging alternative to purchasing a resin interior set. Reference material is a must, along with a great deal of patience as often several attempts at constructing parts are needed until something fits properly. Larger panels and components can be made by first fabricating paper mock-ups that can easily be modified as they are test fitted, and then be used as templates to cut the actual parts from sheet styrene.

Adding and improving detail

By adding and improving the detail of a kit, the hobbyist can enjoy the challenges of creating a unique and more appealing plastic model. Purchasing after-market parts is one way of doing this, but the job can be done with some basic materials and a little ingenuity.

Adding nuts, bolts and screws

Owing to the limits of the injection-moulding process and also the research done by kit manufacturers, nut, bolt and screw detail can often be missing or

A treasure trove of bolt detail can be found on the lower side of a kit's hull. The bolt heads can be sliced off with a sharp hobby blade and used to detail areas of the model that are more visible.

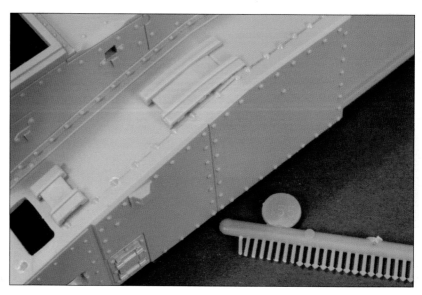

After measuring out the locations of the conical headed rivets for added detail on Tamiya's Char B1 bis, a pencil line was drawn to ensure the row was straight. Grandt Line rivets No. 155 were trimmed from their runner and cemented into place.

incorrectly portrayed on the parts. Reviewing available references can help determine the size, shape and location of the various details, and the inaccurate features can be removed with a sharp hobby knife. Grandt Line is one company that manufactures small railway parts in styrene, including a wide range of nuts, bolts and rivet heads. These tiny mouldings can be shaved from their plastic runner, and, with a very sharp No. 11 hobby blade, picked up and positioned onto a marked spot on a model. For rows of bolts, it's advisable to run a pencil line down a straight edge, or use a piece of marked masking tape to spot the locations of the details to be added.

Underneath the lower hull of many models is a treasure trove of bolt or rivet detail that just begs to be salvaged, since most of it can't be seen on the finished kit. Older, discarded kits are another economical source of valuable details as is, of course, the spare parts bin – nothing should be thrown out when a kit is done with.

Screw-head details can be simulated by pressing a flat-headed syringe needle onto the model's surface to make a round impression, and then pushing the blade of a small jeweller's screwdriver into the middle to create the slot.

Small rivet heads can be formed from thin sheet lead by taking the back end of a drill bit and pressing the sheet through against a soft surface such as a pencil eraser. The resulting concave discs can be manipulated with the tip of a sharp No. 11 blade and cemented into position with crazy glue.

Grab handles

The grab handles on kits tend to be a bit thick, and are often broken when removing them from their runner or when trimming them. Brass rod of an appropriate diameter provides a sturdy replacement. A handy tool available from the US called the Grabhandler is designed as a jig to help bend duplicate metal rod handles of various dimensions. The hobbyist can also achieve acceptable results with a steel ruler and a good pair of pliers or tweezers. To fasten the handles to the model small holes should be drilled into the plastic and the ends of the rod inserted and cemented to the correct height.

Smaller handles can be bent from copper wire or thin solder wire, although solder is somewhat vulnerable to damage. Another detailing tool is the plastic that is used to form the bristles of a typing eraser. These thin filaments can be bent into shape and glued using styrene cement.

After cementing into place, the base of the handles can be treated to simulated welds by adding a small amount of textured epoxy putty.

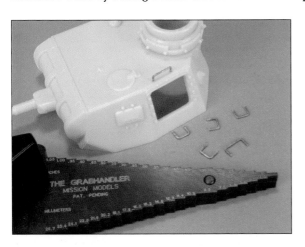

The fragile resin turret grab handles and engine deck hatch handles were replaced with others made from .024in.-diameter brass wire bent to shape using the Mission Models 'Grabhandler'.

Tie-down cleats for the jack-stands on the Char kit were made from copper wire that was bent over a styrene form. Eight identical parts were constructed using this method.

Strapping for the Char B1 bis jack stands and tool stowage was made from thin lead sheet. Buckle detail was added using etched-brass parts from various Aber detail sets.

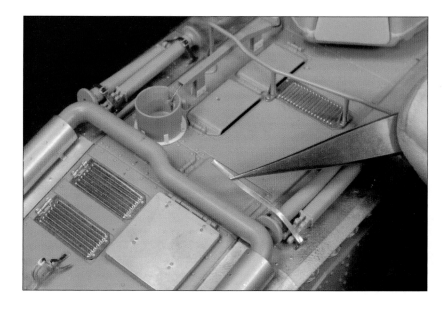

Tool clasps and fasteners

Extremely small items such as fasteners and tool clasps are almost always simplified in styrene and moulded onto the kit parts. By carefully removing the plastic blob that represents the detail, substitute parts made from thin styrene sheet or soft metal can be added for an improved appearance. The after-market tool clasps made from brass are certainly a preference, although they can be difficult to assemble because of their small size and complexity.

Many vehicles have their tools stowed using straps. Strapping can be simulated nicely using soft metal cut into thin strips, and buckles can be added from photo-etched suppliers. The metal can come from commercial sources, or be salvaged from household items like the material covering the top of a wine bottle, a metal tube of adhesive, or aluminium from a disposable ashtray.

Small details

Thinning down the edges of parts can add a realistic touch to the overall look of the kit's detail. Edges of fenders, fighting compartment walls, and vehicle hatches can be scraped down with a sharp hobby knife to a more realistic thickness. The brush guards on some vehicles, like the ones protecting the lights on a Sherman tank, are typically moulded too thickly and need to be carefully trimmed down to a more acceptable appearance.

For the LAV-25 model, SLEP additions include the new gunner's sight with armoured cover and a Platt scissors mount for the M240 machine gun. Weld beads were added to the turret, as well as anti-slip texture.

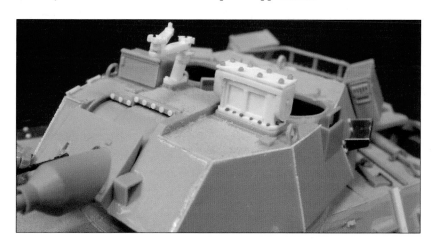

When adding battle damage, parts can be thinned down from the back with a small hobby grinder like a Dremel tool before making the holes with a pin or sharp blade. Heavy wear can be simulated on the tyres of AFVs by taking a grinding tool or hobby knife to the edges.

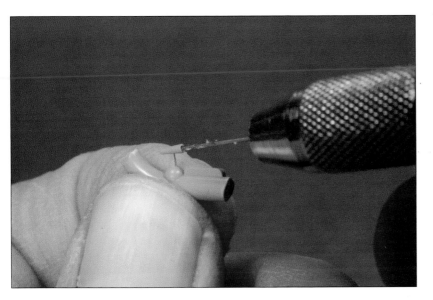

Working on extremely small parts can be difficult, and it occasionally helps to leave them on their styrene runner. The gun barrel of the turret machine gun is getting its muzzle drilled out, which will be trimmed from the runner and glued in place afterwards.

The barrels of machine guns and any other small arms can be drilled out for a more realistic appearance using a miniature drill bit held in a pin vice. The hollow outside edges of hatch hinges can also be drilled out. When spare track links are stowed, the empty locations for the track pins also need to be drilled out.

The 75mm main gun of the Char B1 bis kit was removed with a razor saw to be replaced with a turned aluminium barrel from a detail set from Lion Roar. The cut was kept even and straight to ensure the proper alignment of the gun.

Small springs can be made using very thin copper wire, wrapped around the shaft of a drill bit. These springs can be used as replacements for the plastic examples on the front and rear mudflaps of German Panzer IVs, and the external detail on some American World War II AFV crew hatches.

Headlight lenses can be made from five-minute epoxy, or after-market lenses can be purchased, which are available in various sizes. AFVs often show the signs of damage by having the headlight lenses missing. The headlight reflectors can be enhanced using tin foil or painting them silver.

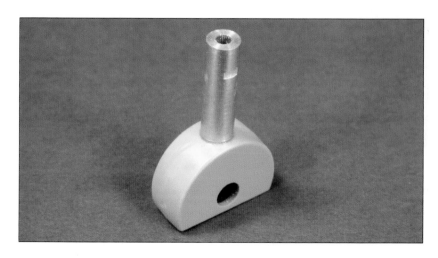

Surface textures and welds
Cast steel surfaces

Rather than feature a smooth surface, most AFVs sport a roughcast look to their steel exteriors. This is especially noticeable on vehicles such as some of the Russian tanks of World War II. Kit manufacturers have recently taken note of this, and have made some reasonable improvements to their kit parts featuring some very well rendered cast steel surfaces.

To roughen up a model's smooth surface, the plastic can be painted with liquid styrene glue or a commercially available lacquer-based product such as Mr Surfacer, and stippled with a stiff brush. Tamiya's Basic Type putty is also good for this type of thing after spreading it onto the surface of the part, wetting it further with liquid cement, and stippling afterwards. Plastic surfaces can also be treated to the burr of a grinder to emulate the marks typical of some cast metal surfaces.

Commercially available products such as Cast-a-Coat, which is a fine-grain, sand-like material suspended in a medium that allows it to be painted onto the surface of the model, can also be used to simulate the rough texture of cast steel.

Weld beads

Model kit manufacturers have made significant improvements in the weld mark detail featured on AFVs. In cases where improvements or additional weld marks are needed, there are a number of options to explore.

An extremely thin length of styrene rod can be positioned and dampened with liquid cement, softening it enough so that it can be pushed and prodded into a rough weld-like texture. This technique is especially helpful in cases where short, small repetitive welds are needed, for example the dust skirt attachment along the sides of a Sherman tank.

Using epoxy putty, sections of weld bead can be added onto a model by forming it into long thin rolls. To ease the placement of the putty, a small groove can be engraved into the plastic with a knife or dental pick, which can also help with welds that have a flush appearance. Dampening the putty with water helps maintain the workability of the material, and allows the texture to be added with a shaped toothpick. To help form the long thin line of the weld, the sides can be straightened by trimming the edges of the length using a No. 11 hobby blade as the putty is textured and flattened down.

Some weld bead appears quite smooth, and can be simulated by running small amounts of white glue into an area masked to the sides with tape. As the glue dries, several layers of fresh glue can be added to achieve the smooth, rippled effect.

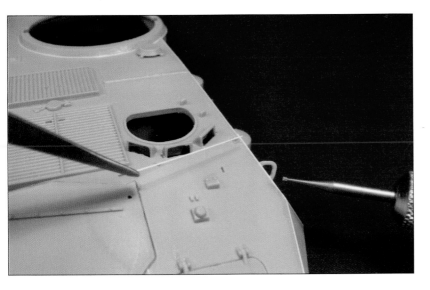

To add the missing weld beads, Plastruct .010in. styrene rod was cemented in place. When dry, a small dovetail bit in a motor tool was used to texture the weld. The gaping holes in the driver's periscopes were later filled with strip styrene.

For gap filling or weld detail, two-part epoxy putty can be rolled into a long thin lump and pressed into place. Aves Apoxie Sculpt was used to fill a joint on the Char's main gun mount.

Since the putty is water soluble, a dampened brush was used to smooth down the joint, with excess putty being scraped away with a hobby blade. The resin detail parts were from the Blast Model set.

Zimmerit

Simulating the texture of *Zimmerit* anti-magnetic paste has long been the challenge of World War II German armour modellers. The paste was a concrete-like mixture applied to AFVs to prevent the adhesion of magnetic mines from late 1943 until September 1944. Various styles of impressions were placed in the material such as ridges, cross-hatch and waffle patterns, depending on the factory that made the vehicle or whether the *Zimmerit* was field applied.

Some model kits are produced with a moulded *Zimmerit* texture, but at present time there are not many in 1/35 scale. After-market manufacturers also produce resin replacement parts for kits with the *Zimmerit* on them, and thin sheets of the pattern that have to be glued onto the kit's surface. Disadvantages

Mori Mori two-part putty along with a sponge and a custom-made rake were used to replicate the *Zimmerit* pattern seen on early Jagdpanthers.

The *Zimmerit* pattern and method of application were tested on a spare Tamiya Jagdpanther hull before applying to the current model.

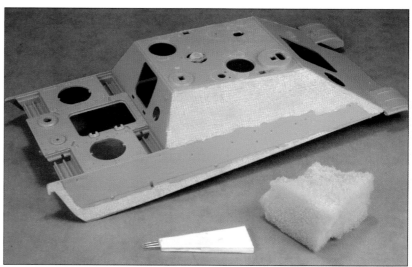

To apply the putty a wide X-Acto chisel blade was used. Care was taken to ensure a thin coat of putty was applied.

Before creating the pattern of small squares in the putty it was sponged to thin it out further and 'roughen' up the texture.

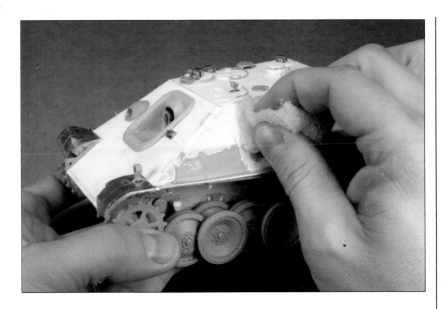

Before mounting the wheels and tracks *Zimmerit* was also applied to the lower hull using the same technique as on the rest of the model.

A close up of the completed *Zimmerit* shows the rough surface and somewhat random pattern of the scored horizontal and vertical lines.

to this are that the pattern is disrupted at a joint on the kit, and it is difficult to simulate the damage and wear that typically occurred to the paste. The pattern of lines on each vehicle's *Zimmerit* was fairly unique, so adding one's own is often a preferred choice.

Adding *Zimmerit* to a German AFV is a fairly involved process and is best handled one small area at a time. Since the paste was added to the actual vehicles after all of the bolts and brackets were in place, it is best to do this at the same stage in the model's assembly. In some cases to simplify construction it may be necessary to change the order of the assembly process, for instance gluing the track cable and brackets onto the *Zimmerit*-coated left hand side of a Tiger I.

Although there have been successful efforts at simulating *Zimmerit* by placing a heated element onto the model's surface and melting the styrene, the preferred method is to use putty that is spread thinly and patterned with various tools. Two-part epoxy putty can be formed by kneading the 'A' and 'B' components together and rolling it into a ball the size of a pea, then spreading it onto the model's surface. The putty should be spread out into a layer as thin as possible, making an effort to keep an even depth of coverage. Since the putty is water soluble, the tools used to spread and texture it can be dampened down so that they don't stick and pull the material from the surface of the model. Care should be taken to place the putty in and around the small details of the kit, and texture it by referring to wartime photos of the actual vehicle. Museum examples of *Zimmerit* on vehicles tend to have post-war applications performed by their staff and are not always authentically reproduced, so caution is advised when using these as a reference.

Adding stowed equipment

The manufacturer typically supplies model kits without a lot of the stowed equipment added by the crews of the actual vehicles. Reference to the photos of real AFVs shows a proliferation of personal gear, extra fuel and ammunition containers, spare road wheels and sandbags. Although it seems to add an element of detail and interest, lengths of chain link were not as common to see slung randomly over AFVs as some modellers like to portray. The tool stowage on some vehicles was occasionally altered by the crew, and reference photos can show just where things were actually fastened down and kept. When adding the equipment to a model, consideration should be given to how the items were fastened down, and how to capture the look of a realistic 'sit' to the items stowed.

A common practice of AFV crews was to use local foliage in an effort to camouflage their vehicles. In addition to adding some historical accuracy to a model, the foliage can add interest by breaking the monotony of a vehicle's appearance with some different colours and texture. Pine boughs are available from Hudson and Allan if a coniferous type of vegetation is preferred, and can be fastened to the model using white glue or contact cement. For the appearance of deciduous foliage, sea foam can be purchased in model railway shops, and dipped into various leafy products from manufacturers such as Noch Trees Lime and Woodland Scenics. Another alternative is a dried plant product called peppergrass, which comes in a wide range of colours, and can be spraypainted any shade of green as required.

Many of the stowage pieces are moulded with large casting plugs. These can be carefully removed with the aid of a jeweller's saw as seen here or, for straight items, scribing and snapping is often easier.

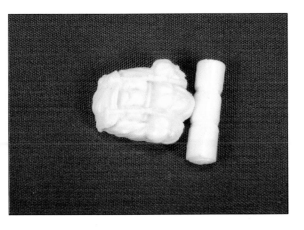

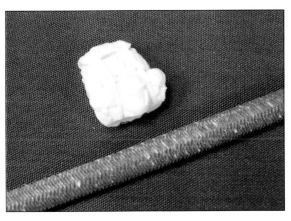

Here are two individual resin stowage pieces, which need to be placed together. Placing them side by side on the model doesn't look very realistic; they need to be modified to look as though they are soft items pushed together.

Here a round rasp is used to create a semicircular depression in the bottom of the pack, which the bedroll will fit into.

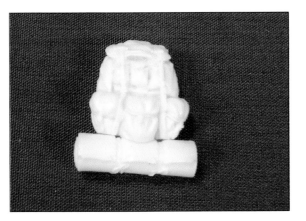

The result looks a little more realistic and is achieved in a matter of minutes.

For a better fit on to the model, a little more drastic surgery is needed. Here the back of a resin pack is hollowed out with a grinding bit in a motor tool.

Some epoxy putty, in this case Aves Apoxie Sculpt, is mixed up and pressed into the hollow. Note how the back has been built up a little to resemble a full pack rather than a flat piece.

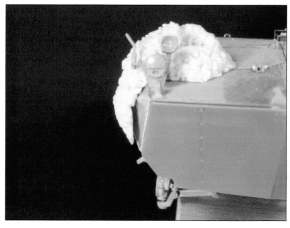

While the putty is still soft, the pack is pressed onto the model. A small amount of petroleum jelly is first brushed on the area where the pack is being place so that it can be removed for painting if necessary.

Although designed for the Trumpeter LAV-25, the Legends camouflage netting leaves an unrealistic gap between the netting and the side of the LAV.

Again, epoxy putty can be used to fill in the gap. A small blob of putty is 'smooshed' under the net, and the excess removed. The net texture is sculpted in with a dental probe in an attempt to match the resin piece.

Visible in this photo are new photo-etched tarp racks and rebuilt tie-downs for stowage straps. Also note the side hatch hinges have been replaced with bits formed from strip styrene, which is more to scale. When adding stowage, it is important to strap everything down; realistic tie-downs help achieve this.

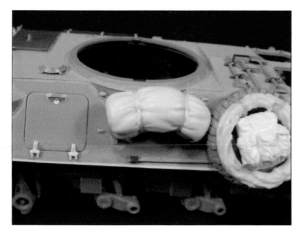
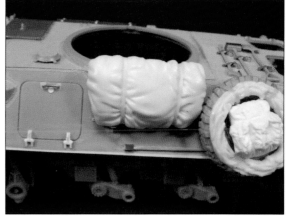

Often commercial resin pieces won't fit the newly improved additions, no matter how much we'd like them to.

In this case, rolling a thin sheet of epoxy putty to the appropriate size makes a new tarp. The tarp is carefully pressed into place while soft, and indentations are sculpted in where tie-down straps will be added. Custom-made stowage can look more realistic and makes your model unique.

Here strips of lead foil have been imbedded in the epoxy putty, rather than trying to attach the strips later. This provides a much stronger attachment obviously.

Painting and finishing

It's the painting process that puts life and realism into the model. Finishing techniques for model kits have been developed over the past 20 years and have taken them from looking like childrens toys to the point where it's hard to tell photographs of the models from the real vehicles. Artistic licence plays a part in the methods used by many modellers to enhance the appearance and detail of the finished piece.

To handle the model during the painting and weathering stages, a file handle with a large wood screw epoxied into the end was attached to the bottom of the model after drilling a small hole to accommodate it.

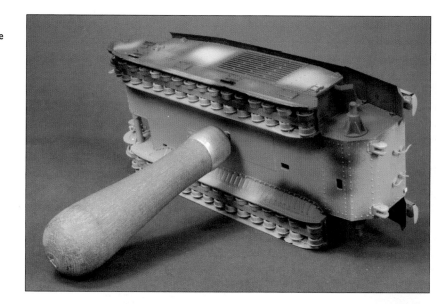

The Char B1 bis model received a dark brown coat of primer paint using Floquil's Roof Brown and some Weathered Black. This was applied using a Paasche H1 airbrush and served as a pre-shade to the camouflage applied afterwards.

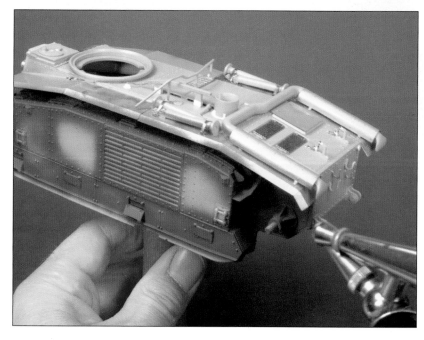

Paint and application

The kit's instruction sheet will indicate some approximate colours for their chosen subjects, which are usually given with reference to a particular line of painting products. It's up to the modeller who has researched the subject to know what colours the model will have, and how they will be applied.

The three basic types of paint used for AFV modelling are enamels, lacquers and acrylics. These can be applied by brush, spray can or airbrush. Enamels and lacquers cover well, but may be affected by subsequent spirit-based washes during the weathering process. Acrylics take more time to apply, but are not affected by the above-mentioned washes.

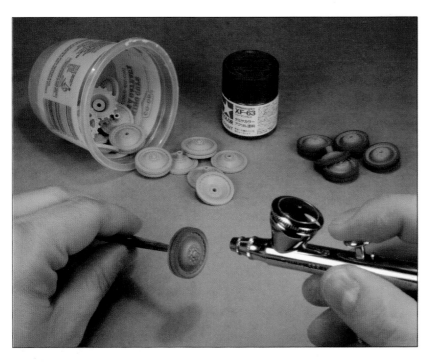

Using Tamiya XF-63 German Grey the rubber portion of the Jagdpanther road wheels were painted before applying the vehicle colour.

Tamiya XF-53 Neutral Grey was applied both to prime the model and provide a neutral starting point for the paint applications to follow.

A 50:50 mixture of Tamiya XF-1 Flat Black and XF-52 Flat Earth was applied to all the recessed or shadowed areas and the lower hull.

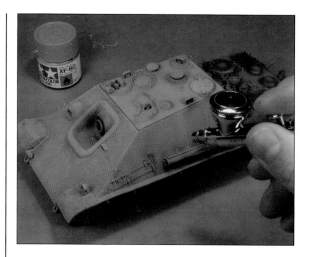

The initial base colour was applied using Tamiya XF-60 Dark Yellow with care taken to ensure the pre-shade colour was still visible.

Over the Tamiya base colour a paint mixture of Vallejo Air 025 Dark Yellow and 074 Radome Tan was applied in a carefully varied pattern.

To create a little variety in the base colour, various items were lightly tinted with a heavily thinned application of Humbrol Super Enamel 081 Pale yellow.

A camouflage pattern of wavy lines was applied using Vallejo Air 041 Tank Brown and 096 Panzer Olive Green 1943.

The camouflage pattern was then toned down with a heavily thinned mixture of Humbrol 083 Ochre. This thinned mixture also unifies the colours.

Airbrush

Although most paint can be applied with a brush, it's quite common for the serious AFV modeller to invest in an airbrush to achieve the desired finishes. The models in this book and the methods described involve airbrush use. The tool is relatively inexpensive, but does need a source of propellant and an area where it can be safely used. A small air compressor is commonly used for supplying the airbrush, and bottled gas can be used which is much quieter but has its own logistical problems of refilling and handling. Spraying paint should occur away from open flames and in a ventilated area so that the fumes do not affect the user and others. Paint must be thinned considerably to spray well from the airbrush. If not, it may spit blobs of the paint onto the model. Experience has shown that the paint to thinner ratio is typically 50:50 for enamels and even thinner for acrylics. Experimenting with various ratios and brands and types of paint can give the modeller a good idea of what works best. Another variable to consider is the air pressure for the airbrush, which can affect the spray pattern.

Although it is possible to paint a completed model as one piece, it is best to separate some of the components of the project for ease of handling and accessibility. It helps to have the turret removed, for example, so that the hull can be manipulated, and if rubber has to be painted onto the road wheels, they can be left off the kit too. It helps to leave off some of the running gear, for instance, to apply dust and dirt onto the hull during the weathering stages.

Primer

The application of a primer coat is an initial step in the process to give a base to the subsequent colours. The surface of the model can then be studied for imperfections and necessary touch-ups that were undetected during construction. Glue marks can be removed, and cracks can be repaired and the primer reapplied. The primer paint also serves to homogenize the surface of the model, which may consist of many types of components, such as various colours of styrene, brass, white metal and resin. In addition, primer can be used to pre-shade a model; by giving the model an initial coat of dark paint, the subsequent base colours can be applied leaving the darker areas as shadow. Primer is typically sprayed onto the model using a can or an airbrush loaded with grey, black or dark-brown enamel or lacquer-based paint. Lacquer paint typically takes a couple of days to dry, much slower than enamel, but is more resilient on the surface.

Painting camouflage

Part of the art of painting scale models is to make them appear how they would look viewed at a relative distance in outside light, in which case their colour would appear lighter than an actual colour 'chip' from the real thing. The base colour of the model is applied after the primer paint has dried completely. To make a slightly lighter shade of the base colour to account for the 'scale effect' of light, some white or light tan can be mixed in with the paint.

After applying the base colour, additional camouflage colours can be applied. The kit's instruction sheet should be used as a reference for the camouflage pattern, or it can be sketched onto a diagram of the model as a painting guide. If a soft-edged scheme is desired, the paint can be airbrushed thinned down to about 30 per cent paint-to-thinner ratio. This should give very fine lines that can be worked onto the edge of the coloured patches or lines. When the outline of the patch of colour has been established, the remainder can be filled in with a wider, more concentrated paint mix. Experimentation with different types of paint should determine the correct dilution ratio for fine lines of camouflage.

The painting of the M113 began with a basecoat in black followed by a mix of Gunze Field Grey and Field Green in a 1:1 ratio. The Gunze paint is semi-gloss acrylic and sprays very well when diluted with Tamiya Thinner.

Tyre Black and Wood Brown were then applied in the standardized NATO camouflage pattern. In retrospect, the brown colour should be darker and with a greater red tone. The Tamiya NATO Brown would have been a better choice.

Eduard Stencils were added for the vehicle call sign.

The glass surfaces were covered with coloured foil, using greenish-blue for the cupola vision ports, and purple and gold for the treated optics.

Weathering consisted of a MiG Productions' 'mud' pigment in the outer edges of the road wheels and 'rust' for the track recesses. The pigments were mixed with Tamiya acrylic thinner, so care must be taken to avoid working them too much as they will lift the paint underneath.

The dust on the hull side was highly diluted Tamiya Buff, sprayed along the lower edge at the front then moving into an upwards curve towards the rear fuel tank. MiG Productions' Black pigment was used for the exhaust soot stains.

Clear red and clear orange paints from Tamiya were used over the top of Testors' Chrome Silver on the brake lights and turn signals. Canada flags came from the Archer Fine Transfers set. The tracks were given a rub of some 6B pencil graphite, which was buffed to a dull shine.

Masking

If some areas of the model are to be kept from being painted then they should be masked off in various ways. Masking tape comes in various forms, but by far the best tape to use is the light yellow tape made specifically for modelling by Tamiya. It has just enough stick not to lift the paint below it, yet it stays where it's placed. The Tamiya tape also leaves no residue on the surface when removed. The wider roll is handy when it comes to masking off the vehicle interior of an open-topped AFV when painting the exterior finish.

Liquid masking compounds are produced by various manufacturers and are painted onto the surface of the model. The thick liquid dries into a rubber-like skin, which is picked off afterwards with a sharp pair of tweezers to reveal the protected paint below. In some cases this compound can be used to create the weathered effect of chipped paint by applying it randomly with an abrasive pad, and then rubbing it off after a second coat of paint has been applied.

Hard-edged camouflage schemes

For hard-edged schemes, there are a couple of approaches. The model can be masked using adhesive tape or liquid masking compound, or the colours can be applied using a paintbrush. Using masking tape is a laborious process and, owing to the surface detail on the model, cannot completely stop some of the

The LAV was primed with black lacquer paint from a spray can. The lacquer paint bonds well to styrene and metal, providing a tough base coat. Some of the paint was decanted into an airbrush jar to touch up any areas that were missed with the more precise control of an airbrush.

The base green was airbrushed on; a 50:50 mix of Tamiya XF-65 Field Grey and Tamiya XF-67 NATO Green. The paint mix was then thinned almost 50:50 with Tamiya thinners for optimum spraying.

The camouflage patterns were brush painted with thinned acrylic paints. This helped to provide a sharp-edged spray pattern without elaborate masking.

Now the patterns were filled in with Tamiya XF-64 Red Brown and XF-69 NATO Black. The main colours were then lightened with XF-57 Buff and the patterns gone over again to highlight some areas.

Several light coats of Future acrylic floor coating were sprayed on to protect the finish from the weathering processes to follow.

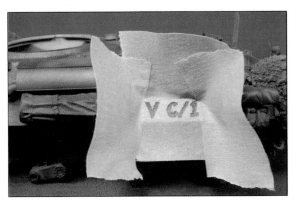

Markings were kept fairly basic; here appropriate stencils have been cut from low-tack painter's masking tape and carefully placed on the model.

Curses! While removing the mask, the paint came off with it, right down to bare plastic. This reinforces the importance of properly cleaning the plastic prior to painting. Luckily the door was easy to remove; it was re-sprayed in the camouflage pattern and the markings sprayed on a second time with no problems encountered.

All stowage items were brush painted prior to further weathering. As they are attached to the vehicle, they would be subject to dust and dirt build-up as well.

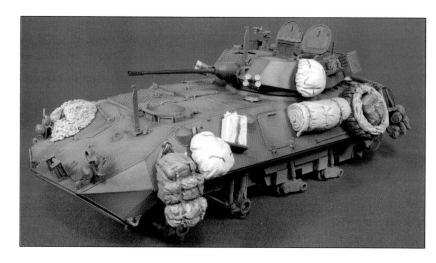

over-spray, which has to be touched up with a paintbrush later. Low-tack masking tape has to be used for this process, since regular tape can lift the paint when it's removed. To cut the sections of tape for masking, spread it out on a piece of glass or ceramic tile and then sketch the rough outline of the camouflage patch onto it. A sharp No. 11 hobby blade can then be used to follow the sketched line smoothly and remove the piece to be placed on the model.

After spray-painting the hard-edged scheme onto the model, the tape should be removed when the paint is still wet to reduce the chance of a hardened 'lip' of paint forming at the edge of the tape. If there are a few different colours to add to the base, the procedure is repeated until all of the painting is complete, leaving time for the previous coat to dry. At the end of the airbrushing, there may be some over-sprayed areas where it was difficult for the tape to adhere. These spots can be touched up with a paintbrush to complete the look of the hard-edged camouflage.

To paint the scheme with a brush after the initial base colour has been applied, the subsequent camouflage patches should be spread on with a large wide brush using paint with a dense pigment. Alternately, the camouflage demarcation line can be painted in place with a brush giving the pattern the necessary hard edge; the rest of the colour can be added with an airbrush, taking care to minimize any over-spray.

Painting the smaller details

Before the bulk of the weathering process is started, all of the vehicle's small details should be painted. Lights, vehicle tools, tyres, antennae and exhausts should all be completed so that they weather down with the rest of the entire model.

For improvised painting pallets many disposable household items can suffice. To mix and apply a small amount of paint the lid of a plastic yogurt container works well, along with a plastic lined bottle cap. For applying washes at a later stage, oil paint can be smeared onto a small sheet of polyethylene and mixed with thinners.

Handles of the shovels, pickaxes, etc. can be picked out in a wood colour, and then have a darker brown added in the form of woodgrain pattern. Stowed tools were sometimes painted the same colour as the body of the vehicle, and references should be checked to confirm this type of thing. Metal components of the tools can be painted either matt black or steel and then dry-brushed with a small amount of silver enamel mixed with raw umber oil paint to give them a metallic sheen.

Rubber tyres on a tank's road wheels or a wheeled AFV are rarely a black colour. In most cases these should be painted with a dark grey. The tyres can then be dry-brushed with an earth-coloured enamel, followed by an even lighter highlighting of Humbrol Khaki Drill. Another method of weathering the tyres is to paint on a mixture of dirt-coloured pastel chalk dust, then rub some of it off with a finger, allowing the recesses of the detail to keep the dirt ingrained.

Painting exhausts and mufflers

When AFVs have been painted, the exhaust pipes and mufflers initially end up the same colour as the rest of the vehicle. Soon after they enter service, the heat takes its toll on the paint, which turns dark, breaks off and starts to show the effects of oxidization, including rust. By studying the look of mufflers on actual AFVs, the colours and rust patterns on the exhaust systems can be replicated in miniature. It's not uncommon to see pictures of vehicles that still have sections of the original paint on their mufflers, with certain areas displaying the effects of heat. The patterns of rust tend to be spotted and patchy.

Exhaust pipes can be painted in a light tan with some rust colour added, creating an almost pinkish look. To this is added some very small random spots of dark brown. The adjoining muffler, which starts in the base colour of the vehicle, can have some patchy areas of dark brown painted onto it, but leaving a bit more of the original colour showing than on the exhaust pipe. Over this, various lighter browns and earth colours of chalk pastel powder can be brushed on, with a hint of orange pastel here and there to simulate a rusty appearance. As the chalk pastel dust is spread around, it blends the appearance of the exhaust system, which develops a realistic look. Only near the end of the exhaust pipe would there appear to be any black soot.

Painting tracks

New all-metal track links tend to be a very dark colour, but quickly start to fade in appearance when placed on a vehicle. When studying the colour of track links on construction equipment, they tend to take on the appearance of the ground they travel on, with a slight metallic sheen at the points of contact with the ground and running gear. To replicate this with model tank tracks, the runs should be initially painted with a dark grey or dark earth enamel. Following this, powdered earth-tone pastel chalks mixed with Tamiya's acrylic paint thinner are daubed onto the tracks, using the same colours that will be used for the groundwork that the model will sit on, and also be weathered with. A mix of darker and lighter tones will give the track runs some variety of colour. Using a cloth dampened with the Tamiya thinner, the pastel mixture can be rubbed

The ModelKasten tracks were first painted with Tamiya XF-63 German Grey, over the top of this were randomly applied patches of XF-57 Buff and XF-52 Flat Earth.

Thinned with isopropyl alcohol, Tamiya XF-63 German Grey was painted onto the inside portion of the tracks where the rubber tyres would run.

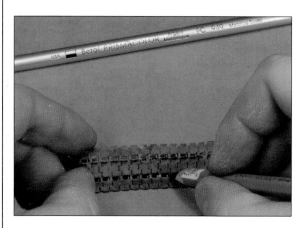

Prismacolor HB and silver pencils were used to simulate the wear from the drive sprocket teeth on the inside face of the tracks.

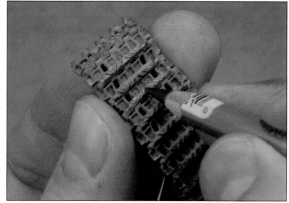

These same pencils were also used to simulate the wear on the track face. The HB pencil was applied to the main face of the track only.

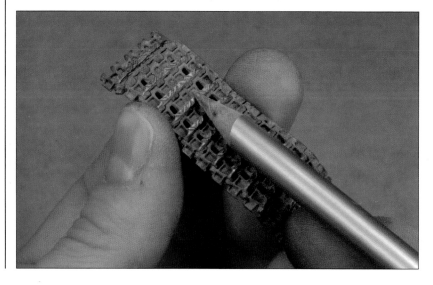

The silver Prismacolour pencil was then applied to the high points on the track face.

off the points of contact where the track links would show bare metal. Silver- and steel-coloured enamel paint can then be mixed with a bit of raw umber oil paint and dry-brushed onto the high points of the track links to simulate the bare metal associated with ground contact and the areas rubbed clean by the running gear.

Application of markings and decals

Researching the colour schemes of AFVs also allows the modeller to decide upon the markings that will be added to the vehicle. Tactical numbers, unit and divisional insignia, and personal markings are a few examples of the things to add. The choice to add markings before, after, or during the weathering stages can be made on a project-by-project basis, since various techniques can either harm the markings or accentuate the appearance of things like decal film. The modeller should keep in mind that the decals should appear to have the same amount of weathering as the rest of the model.

If the kit manufacturer has supplied a variety of decals it can help with the choices. As the modeller builds up an inventory of kits, the pool of decal sheets expands to include those that can be 'stolen' from future or previous builds. Numerous after-market companies produce sheets of markings in either water-slide or rub-on form. These after-market products tend to be well researched and produced on beautifully thin carrier film.

To prepare a model for the application of water-slide decals, the surface should be made glossy. This prevents the formation of 'silvering' – trapped air under the decal surface. The areas where the markings are to be applied should be airbrushed with clear gloss, which is then allowed to dry thoroughly before the markings are added. After the decals have soaked in warm water for about 30 seconds, they can be tested for free movement before being lifted from the paper backing. A drop or two of water on the receiving surface can help with orienting the decal after it has been positioned on the surface of the model. Once the decal is in its correct location, it can be lightly pressed down with a dampened cloth to squeeze out the water underneath. A special decal setting solvent, for example 'Solvaset', can be placed onto the decal to help it form over surface detail. Caution has to be exercised with this liquid, since it starts to weaken the structure of the decal and sometimes results in its destruction if it is moved too much. When the decal and the surrounding surface have completely dried, the area can be airbrushed with a clear, flat medium, restoring a homogeneous finish to the model.

Rub-on markings have the advantage of being able to be placed onto the model's surface without the requirements of gloss and then flat finishes. The markings have to be placed onto a flat surface, since they are next to

After painting the camouflage colours of brown and green onto the Char BI model, areas where the decals were to be applied were sprayed with Tamiya's clear acrylic gloss. Echelon's decals for 'Nancy II' of the 37e BCC were applied using Solvaset decal setting solution. This liquid softens the decal material and allows it to form itself over undulations on the model's surface.

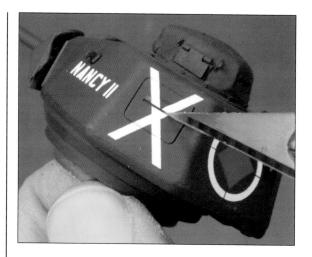

After the decals had dried, the areas were airbrushed with a flat finish, and the excess decal film was trimmed away from the hatch openings with a sharp blade.

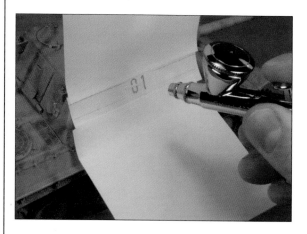

Weathering of the model started by applying Vallejo Model Color 978 Dark Yellow and 976 Buff, which were mixed together at various ratios and applied around areas of wear.

To create the numbers for the Jagdpanther a custom stencil was made using a Post-It note. Vallejo Air 001 White was sprayed at a low air pressure to try and reduce any paint overspray.

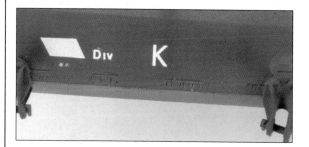

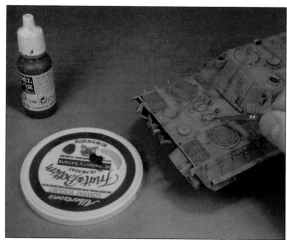

For the markings on the Panzerbefehlswagen III, the letter 'K', which signified the division was attached to Gruppe von Kleist, is from an old Letraset dry transfer sheet. The letters that make up 'Div' were part of the copyright statement in the border of that sheet. The divisional insignia, two yellow dots, is from a Microscale decal sheet that was included with one of the Kagero Photosniper books. The white rhomboid, the tactical sign for a Panzer division, was cut from a white decal sheet.

Vallejo Model Color 872 Chocolate Brown was applied on its own and over the top of the previous mixture of 978 Dark Yellow and 976 Buff.

impossible to adapt to any significant surface detail. To place a marking of this type, they are cut from the sheet and oriented with the help of tape onto the surface of the model. It is crucial to get the alignment correct on these markings because there is no playing around with it afterwards. The marking should then be rubbed onto the surface from the back with an object such as a ballpoint pen, starting at one side and working to the other. It takes experience to know how much pressure to apply and some experimentation is advisable. The backing should then be pulled back and should reveal the entire marking now on the model.

The ambitious modeller can also produce their own markings by painting them on. Details such as hatches, periscopes and vision flaps create a surface problematic for the application of pre-made markings. With thinly taped lines and pencil dots as a guide, and using a steady hand, the markings can be painted in using a fine brush. A marking can also be sprayed onto the model using an airbrush and masking process.

Weathering

Weathering an AFV model has developed into a hobby of its own. With the basic paint scheme of a model completed, the weathering process takes the model from its simplistic look to a realistic miniature. The process involves not only making the vehicle look dirty, but also accentuates shade and highlight. It adds wear and tear, dust, marks, splashes and fading. There are many techniques that the modeller can draw upon to produce a finished model weathered to their satisfaction. If several components of the model have not been added to the main assembly, it's important to make sure that each of these items gets the same weathering treatment.

The first stages of weathering have been started if the model has been pre-shaded during initial painting. To further emphasize the shading and highlighting aspect of the paint job, a lighter colour of the base paint can be mixed by adding a light tan or buff to the base colour, and airbrushed onto the model in areas that would fade because of wear or sunlight. The effect should accent the patches of colour on the camouflage scheme, and the separate features of a single colour vehicle. The paint should be thinned sufficiently (10 per cent paint to thinner mix) to make the tonal change in the paint finish quite subtle.

Dust and dirt

One of the first steps to take when weathering an AFV model is to apply a layer of dust and dirt to the paint finish. This step serves to make the vehicle look

The metal portions of the vehicle tools were painted with Humbrol Metalcote 27003 Polished Steel. This paint was then buffed to provide a realistic metal sheen. A silver Prismacolor pencil was then used to highlight various edges of the tools.

The vehicle exhaust pipes were first painted various red and pink shades using Vallejo Model Colors. On top of this, light applications of Mig Productions' pigments P024 Light Rust and P029 Brick Dust were applied.

The Befehlswagen was sprayed with Lifecolor UA207 RAL 7021 Schwarzgrau Panzergrau acrylic paint followed by application of the decals. A dusty coat mixed from highly thinned Tamiya XF-52 Flat Earth, XF-51 Khaki Drab and XF-57 Buff was then sprayed over the entire model, concentrating on the lower areas where most build-up would occur.

To begin the weathering process, the Char B1 bis was airbrushed with a coat of dirt-coloured acrylic paint. Diluted Tamiya Buff was sprayed over the entire model to emulate accumulated dust, concentrating on areas that would show the most build-up like the sides and rear end.

For a different approach to weathering the LAV-25, a slurry was made from dust-coloured pigments and low odor paint thinners. This was liberally brushed over the entire model and force dried with a hair drier. It looked quite horrible at this stage, but not to worry, most of it will be removed.

A soft, wide brush was used to brush off most of the pigment. The types of brush used can be varied depending on how much pigment needs to be removed. A soft cloth can also be used for flat surfaces

A clear flat acrylic, in this case Polly Scale Clear Flat, was airbrushed on to seal and protect the pigment. Keep in mind a clear coating, whether gloss, semi-gloss, or even flat will lessen the 'dust' effect of dry pigments.

The tyres were given a light overspray of Tamiya Buff, the majority of which was quickly wiped off to leave the lighter colour in the recesses. The hubs were also given a pigment dust treatment. Black pigments were then rubbed onto the tread surfaces.

like it's been used, and to give an initial 'toning down' to the paint scheme and markings. It also helps to simulate the effect of outside light on the model.

By airbrushing a very diluted mixture of light buff or tan paint onto key areas of the kit, it places a realistic pattern of dirt into areas around the running gear, rear plate, fenders and anywhere that this would accumulate as the real vehicle drove over a dusty terrain. The paint should be placed everywhere on the model, but concentrated heaviest in the areas which would accumulate most, such as the running gear and rear of the vehicle. If certain areas are missed, they become painfully clear in photos of the finished work.

For heavier deposits of dirt, chalk pastel or other types of pigment powders can be placed in and around the running gear and up and under the lower hull, and then soaked with Tamiya's acrylic thinner to adhere them in place. Several different colours can be used to simulate wet or dry earth. Acrylic paste can be mixed with these powders and also 'static grass' to create a thicker mud that can also be strategically placed around the vehicle's wheels and suspension components. By studying photos of real vehicles, it becomes obvious where dirt specifically accumulates. This step is made easier if the wheels have not yet been permanently attached to the model. The wheels themselves should also show signs of a muddy build-up if this has been applied to the vehicle's hull. Typically, the tread surface of the road wheel tyres would be clean owing to the constant contact they have with the inner track surface, so an effort should be made to keep the muddy mixture from this area.

On the Char B1 bis model, ground pastel chalk was piled into the areas in behind the running gear to emulate the buildup of dirt that would have accumulated on a well used AFV.

Washes

Applying a 'wash' to a model refers to adding diluted paint to the surface. There are a number of effects that can be created by this method. To enhance detail and shadow, a dark paint wash can be brushed onto the model's finish. Because of its fine pigment, oil paint is

Tamiya's acrylic thinner was soaked up with a large paintbrush and allowed to wick into the pastel dust, holding the material in place when dry.

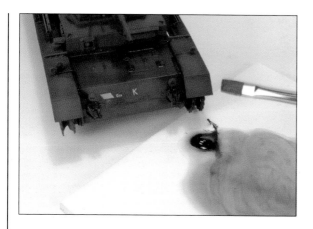

A very thin wash of black artist's oil paint mixed with paint thinner was applied to the model. Paint thinner was used instead of turpentine as it dries flat and does not leave tidemarks on the surface as it dries. Gently blowing on the surface helps speed up the drying process.

Demonstrating the technique on the Char B1 bis model, this was done one section at a time, and the paint was specifically applied to the nooks, crannies and engraved detail of the model

typically thinned down with mineral spirits and added with a fine-tipped brush to a pre-soaked surface, which allows the paint to be 'wicked' into the cracks and crevices of the model. The general area of the model should be wetted with the mineral spirit to avoid getting tidemarks left over when the wash dries. If the base paint used was an acrylic then there is less likelihood of the mineral spirit wash ruining the finish.

A wash of a light-coloured paint can be used to tone down the look of a paint scheme by giving it an apparent layer of dirt. The paint pigment that gathers in the recesses of the model's surface detail in this case would resemble accumulated dust.

The wash can also serve to add a tonal change to the overall painted look. If the thinned paint is spread over the entire surface of the model it can change the appearance of a dark yellow finish, for instance, into a deeper, richer hue. Sometimes referred to as applying a filter, oil paint can be diluted with mineral spirits and added in several layers to achieve the tone desired. Pre-packaged 'filters' can be purchased from MIG Productions, with the paints already thinned for the modeller's convenience.

Pastel chalk and earth-coloured pigment were brushed onto the model's exterior in a streaked fashion, emphasizing the dirt build-up that was typical of these vehicles in heavy service. Localized washes of thinned, black oil paint were repeated in some spots on top of the dusty exterior to show stains from oil, grease and grime.

Stains and streaks

When the model's surface is dampened with thinner during the wash stage, it provides an opportunity to add some streaks and stains to the model. The effect of rust, dust and rain can leave vertical marks on the painted surfaces of an AFV, and, although the effect is more artistic licence than fact, it enhances the appearance of a weathered model.

Small spots of oil paint are placed in various locations on the painted surface that has been slightly dampened with mineral spirit. The suggested colours would typically be burnt sienna or raw umber. The paint is dragged downwards using a dampened brush with care to keep the direction perpendicular to the ground.

Wartime photos of the Char B1 bis show a heavy amount of oil streaks in various locations on the vehicle sides, possibly from the lubricated running gear. Adding thin lines of Lifecolor's Tensocrom acrylic oil simulated these oil streaks.

For a faded effect, various colours of oil paint can be added to the finish. Small dots of whites and yellows can be dabbed onto a khaki green base colour for example, and blended in, creating a subtle weathering effect.

Dry-brushing

The technique of dry-brushing involves taking a minimum amount of paint pigment on a brush and lightly applying it to an area on the model so that the raised detail picks up the paint. Typically used to add lighter colours to enhance details, dry-brushing can also be used to add darker paint if required. Like many weathering processes, this one takes some experience to achieve a pleasing result, and is easy to overdo.

The teeth on the drive sprockets of the model were rubbed with a mixture of silver enamel toned down with raw umber oil paint. Most of the paint was rubbed off onto a paper card, and the remaining pigment dry-brushed into place.

To highlight the features of a model, a lighter shade of the base colour is placed on a paintbrush, which is wiped down to ensure a minimum quantity is contained in the bristles. A good quality brush, such as sable hair, will give the best results with this method. The brush is then rubbed onto the model's surface – lightly at first, then with more pressure as the effect becomes apparent. By repeating the process with an even lighter colour on a smaller section of the same area of the model, the effect is enhanced. The pigment of the paint used should be fairly dense, and typically the best paint to use is the thick material at the bottom of a tin of Humbrol enamel.

Adding white paint to lighten a base colour is not necessarily the best thing to do in many cases, as it can give an odd-looking tone to the finished result. Dark green or grey can be lightened with tan and buff, and black can be lightened with tan and flesh colours, so it is good to experiment and see what others have used successfully.

Metal highlights can also be added with the dry-brushing method. Areas of the vehicle that have had the paint worn down to the steel show a gleam that can be simulated with a steel colour. Humbrol Silver and Steel can be combined and toned down with a small amount of raw umber oil paint, then dry-brushed onto areas such as around crew hatches, walkways and other places of high traffic. It is quite important to subdue the bright appearance of the silver paint, since bare metal at that scale would otherwise appear too garish.

A small template made from sheet styrene was used to paint the spare track link chevron wear marks on the hull sides.

The centre of each chevron wear mark was filled in with Vallejo Model Color 872 Chocolate Brown. On top of this a small spot of 502 Abteilung Oil Color ABT-070 Dark Rust was applied and then dragged down with mineral spirits.

Dark brown patches were randomly painted onto the muffler shrouds to show evidence of rust in various places. This was later treated to a brushing of lighter coloured pastel powders to even out the look, and give the effect of heat on the paint.

Chipped paint and scratches were applied to the upper part of the hull using Floquil's Weathered Black. The random effect of the chips helps to add interest to the overall look of the model, and is more artistic license than how it actually would have appeared.

Paint chipping

Simulating chipped paint on a model can enhance detail and emulate heavy wear on the vehicle's finish. When paint is removed from the steel, the marks can show bare metal, primer, rust, or a previous layer of paint.

Small random spots of paint can be dotted onto the model in the areas most likely to exhibit scratches and wear. The spots should have predominantly jagged edges not applied with any kind of uniformity or obvious pattern. It is helpful to study construction vehicles to see how the abuse of the painted exterior appears, and to mimic this in miniature. This weathering feature can very easily be overdone, and some restraint should be exercised when applying the paint chips.

An alternate method of applying the chipped paint look to a model is to wet a piece of abrasive pad or 'Scotch Brite' with paint, remove the excess and then press the pad onto the model in the required areas. It is best to test this method first to determine the right amount of paint and pressure to apply to achieve the desired effect.

Coloured pencils

In addition to dry-brushing bare metal highlights onto the model, coloured pencils can also be applied to some surfaces. On the edges of road wheels where they make contact with the tracks, a silver pencil can be run around the raised lip to indicate recent wear. Soft lead pencils are also good for showing a more subdued look to these areas of the model, with a number 2H being ideal. Track links can also be touched up in this fashion.

The guide teeth were also highlighted with a chisel point metallic silver pencil crayon to reproduce the wear from constant contact with the road wheels and idler. The links were supported on a piece of styrene strip wrapped with a piece of tissue paper to protect the pastel chalk finish.

Presentation

Planning the diorama

AFV models lend themselves ideally to placement in a small diorama or vignette. There is a near-limitless availability of figures, buildings and all of the associated accessories. To plan the construction of an AFV kit on a base, the modeller has to strike a balance between historical accuracy and artistic licence.

The time period in which the AFV served needs to relate to the surrounding terrain, road signs, ground conditions and building structures. The uniforms

To prepare the layout of the eventual diorama, the planning starts early in the construction of the models. The kits were placed in their approximate locations to check for balance, symmetry and viewing appeal. A 14 × 10in. piece of .75in. plywood with a section of carved polystyrene provided the base.

The tow chains of the vehicle were painted with Floquil's Weathered Black, and then given a wash with dirt-coloured pastel chalks mixed with Tamiya's acrylic thinner. Some orange pastel chalk dust was also brushed onto the links to show a suggestion of rust.

ABOVE German infantrymen were built from various DML figure sets and modified with detailed resin heads from Hornet and Warriors. The figures were mounted on wooden toothpicks to ease handling during painting. The faces and hands were primed with Tan enamel n preparation for painting with artists oils.

After painting the figures' faces and hands with artist's oils, the uniforms were airbrushed flat black. Enamels were used to paint the field grey tunics and trousers using a dry-brush technique. Humbrol's No. 111 Uniform Grey was mixed with varying amounts of olive green, black and khaki drill and then dry-brushed onto the figures allowing the black base to act as a pre-shadow. The details on the weapons and insignia were painted in using Vallejo acrylics and a fine-tipped 000 brush.

and weapons of the figures also need to coincide with the period of the event depicted. Although not essential, the direction in which the vehicles face should perhaps be considered in the mind's eye when laying out the models on the base, for instance German tanks would presumably face to the right if advancing on the Russian front.

Multiple crew figures, or figures which will be positioned on or near the model, need to relate to each other or a have a common focus. This will provide the vignette or diorama with symmetry and balance. To make the figures in a scene interact may involve re-positioning their heads and limbs. It is best to do this during the preliminary planning stages of the AFV model's construction, since things like hatches, tools and other elements of the vehicle need to be coordinated with the placement of figures.

The size of the base should be determined in the early stages of the kit's construction, with space allowed for any buildings, trees and other defining structures. To give a further element of interest, the base can be 'stepped' by adding a second level to the groundwork. It is also wise to give thought to where the model will be displayed and how it may need to be transported to modelling events and club meetings, etc. It is not uncommon to want to take a finished diorama to a display, only to find out that it won't fit into any available box.

As the models begin to take shape and the other aspects of the diorama are built, test fitting the components throughout the process will give the modeller a feel for how the end result is developing. The overall layout can be improved by revising the initial plan. The finished scene should become a combination of a good plan with some fine adjustments along the way. One of the golden rules of creating a diorama is to try not to place any of the components of the scene parallel to the front. When using sections of cobblestone street this can be difficult to manage, but the result makes it worth cutting the sections at an angle.

Bases

Bases for dioramas are generally a piece of .75in. plywood cut to fit the planned scene, which is finished later with a decorative edging. Another possibility is a pre-finished trophy plaque, although these tend to be expensive. Models can be positioned to overhang the edge of the base, but it is generally safer to position most of the vehicles, figures and other components at least half an inch inside the edge to prevent damage during transport.

The surface of the wooden base has to be prepared for groundwork to be added. If a pre-finished piece of wood is used, the finish has to be sanded down to give something for the groundwork to adhere to.

Urban dioramas

City or town scenes involve a fair investment in time and effort. The armoured vehicle and figures are now joined by the construction, painting and weathering of buildings and street accessories, some of which can be more elaborate than the actual AFV itself. It is important to keep the focus of the scene on the subject vehicle, and not have it lost amongst overshadowing structures.

There are many products available to help create an urban setting. Building kits made of resin and plaster are offered by numerous after-market manufacturers, along with such accessories as street lights, petrol pumps, water fountains, telegraph poles, etc. Typically an AFV scene in a destroyed area of a city would include a fair amount of debris and rubble, and this, too, can be purchased. Some manufacturers also offer entire bases complete with buildings, street details and rubble cast in resin. The ambitious modeller can also fabricate many of the items mentioned using foam board and other hobby construction materials. Sacrificing convenience for economics, a number of household items can be used to help in the fabrication of a diorama. The placement of small detailed items can add interest to the overall scene, such as household furniture, books or papers, posters, signs or even a small pet animal.

While collecting research for the LAV-25 project, it was decided to incorporate two figure sets available from Warriors to make a small vignette. Often the type of figures available will determine if any changes need to be made to the kit during construction.

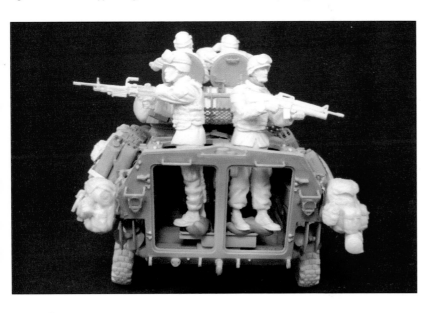

Test fitting the figures to the vehicle before painting and finishing is important to make sure the figures will have a natural appearance. Here it was determined that the rear crew members would be standing too high, so some adjustment will need to be made. The wheels appear crooked, as they have just been loosely placed on the axles.

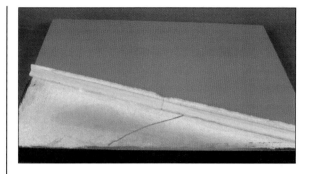

ABOVE LEFT The base is a piece of MDF (medium density fibreboard) sealed with Varathane. The curb was cut from green florist's foam and coated with a few layers of thinned wood glue. The asphalt side is simply Rustoleum textured grey paint sprayed directly from the can on to the base.

ABOVE RIGHT Groundwork was added by sprinkling Polyfilla with assorted sand and small pebbles. Evergreen 'I' beams were placed in the still-wet groundwork. Prior to adding the Polyfilla, the base edges were masked with several layers of tape to provide containment.

ABOVE A white motorway shoulder stripe was masked and sprayed on. Groundwork was sprayed a suitable desert earth colour, and a little grass was added for interest (made from deer hair available at fly-fishing supply shops). Lastly, the base edges were painted gloss black.

The finished vignette. This represents a LAV in a convoy that has pulled over and stopped to check out a suspicious area. It is important to note all the stowage has been strapped or tied down to avoid the magical magnetic stowage effect sometimes seen on models.

The finished Panzerbefehlswagen III model was attached to a base and crewed with figures from the Dragon Models 'German Tank Crew 1939–1943' kit 6375.

After the buildings and other accessories to be used for the scene are constructed, they should be painted and weathered using similar methods to those for AFV models. It is important to note that concrete is a tan colour and not grey. Building bricks look best if some of the individual ones are picked out in a different hue than the overall dark reddish brown, and adding the light-coloured mortar between them adds an element of realism.

Rural dioramas

A diorama in a rural setting is generally simpler to complete than an urban one. A scene can be completed within a day or so, allowing some overnight drying before the final stages. Model railway shops carry a good range of material for putting together some very convincing miniature terrain: pre-made trees for all seasons, grass of all lengths and colours, plus selections of grit and gravel. Foliage and other vegetation are also available from various hobby manufacturers made from etched brass, laser-cut paper and resin.

To begin construction of a rural-style diorama, a mixture of groundwork should be prepared and spread onto the base in a thin layer. This mixture

A papier-mâché mixture of Celluclay, acrylic paint, water and white glue was mixed up and spread onto the base of the diorama as thinly as possible. The material shrinks drastically when it dries, and the polystyrene needed to be firmly adhered to the wooden base to keep from being lifted at the edges.

After adding some fine-grain sand and small stones to the road area, static grass was applied to the lower section and prodded around with a stiff brush. Sections of kit tracks were placed into the wet groundwork to make impressions in which to place the models, and to show tracks from previous traffic.

Woodland Scenics 'Fine Leaf Foliage' provided the trees that were glued into place on the edge of the roadway. By placing the models temporarily on the base during this stage, the overall look of the scene can be judged as the trees are arranged. Small sections of Heki grass matt were teased apart and white-glued into place in a random fashion.

Dragon Models Panzer IVC was added to the scene to create a historical event involving the Pz.Rgt. 31 of 5.Panzer Division who saw action against the 37e BCC of the French 1ere Division Blindée near Denée, Belgium, in May 1940.

The German infantrymen inspect the abandoned Char B1 bis while the crew of the victorious Panzer look on. To tone down the look of the various components of the groundwork, a diluted coat of Tamiya Buff was airbrushed onto the base before the models and figures were added.

generally consists of a papier-mâché type of material and can shrink as it dries, so any foam board used to elevate a section of the base needs to be glued or screwed down tightly. The shrinking groundwork can lift itself from the base if not adhered well enough, so unfinished wood and plenty of white glue is necessary to ensure the material stays put. If a pre-finished base is used, the edges should be masked off with tape for protection.

With the ground cover still wet, some fine grit can be placed randomly around the entire base concentrating on roadways and paths. The material can be patted down to stay in the groundwork making sure that the larger pieces of grit do not end up under the AFV's tracks or wheel imprints. Static grass of an appropriate colour for the season depicted should now be added by pinching clumps of the material and pushing it randomly into the wet ground cover. Prodding the grass with a stiff bristled brush can help it stand up, enhancing the effect.

Vinyl track runs from other kits or spare wheels mounted as a roller can be used to make impressions in the damp groundwork as if from passing vehicles and also the track marks from the AFV that is to be mounted onto the base.

Trees, shrubs and other types of foliage should next be placed into the diorama, along with other accessories such as fences, signposts or other structures. It helps to place the model into position when arranging the components of the scene since balance and symmetry are important to the overall look. Consideration should also be given to positioning things correctly in order not to obscure significant details and hours of modelling effort. After drilling small holes in the base, the foliage stems can be inserted and cemented into position along with the other items using white glue. Figures can be secured to the base by drilling holes into the bottoms of their feet and inserting a section of a metal paper clip, and then gluing that into a corresponding hole in the diorama base.

To blend the scene together before the models are added, the base should be lightly sprayed with a thinned mixture of dust-coloured paint. Diluted Tamiya Buff sprayed at a low pressure setting on the airbrush can be added to various areas that need to have a stark look toned down.

As a final touch to an unfinished plywood base edge, a decorative material should be cut to cover it. Wood veneer strips can be purchased that feature an adhesive surface, or artist matte board can be cut into sections and white-glued into place.

Regardless of skill level, one's abilities improve with each model built. The fundamentals of modelling that this book describes are useful to either novices or experienced modellers and each project is an opportunity to try new ideas. The contributors to this book hope that you will be inspired to use some of their techniques and tips that, when applied, may reward you with better modelling results, and more satisfaction in the hobby.

Front left to right, Tom Cockle, Graeme Davidson, Jim Carswell, Steve van Beveren and Gary Edmundson.

Index